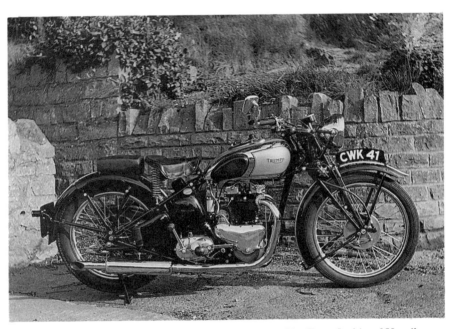

Edward Turner's 1937 Prototype Model T restored by Dave Jenkin of Yeovil.

TRIUMPH

Speed Twin

The development history of the pre-unit & unit construction 500cc twins

H. Woolridge

Foulis

Haynes
®

ISBN 0 85429 722 7

© **Harry Woolridge 1989**

First published September 1989

A FOULIS Motorcycling Book

British Library Cataloguing in Publication Data
Woolridge, Harry
    Triumph speed twin.
    1. Speed twin motorcycles. History. Triumph
    I. Title
    629.2'275

    ISBN 0-85429-722-7

Library of Congress Catalog Card No. 89-84299

Published by
Haynes Publishing Group
Sparkford, Nr. Yeovil. Somerset BA22 7JJ, England

Haynes Publications Inc
861 Lawrence Drive, Newbury Park, California 91320 USA

Editor: Jeff Clew
Cover design: Syd Guppy
Printed in England by J.H. Haynes & Co. Ltd.

INTRODUCTION

Now that the fiftieth anniversary of the Triumph Speed Twin has passed it seems appropriate to commit a few details of the machine to print. The Speed Twin was one of Triumph's most successful models and was certainly the forerunner of all other Triumph Twins.

In this book I have attempted to give a factual account of the Speed Twin history/specification. This, I feel, will be most useful to the restorer/owner who wishes to ensure his or her machine is correct for its year.

Maybe a word on Triumph seasonal production procedure would not go amiss and so avoid any arising confusion. It was for some years Triumph's policy to introduce their next year's models around October/November of the preceding year. This will be noted in the build dates accompanying the years. Towards the late 1960s this date was brought forward even more and a July start for the next year was not unknown.

Harry Woolridge

Harry Woolridge
Weddington,
Nuneaton.
July 1988

Acknowledgements

The author wishes to record his appreciation to his wife Barbara, and Mrs. C.M. Gibbs, for the patience shown in setting out and typing the original manuscript.

PART ONE

Company History

The Triumph Cycle Company was originally started in London by two young Germans in the late 1800s. The Company was an import/export business selling bicycles and the Triumph brand name was chosen as it was self-explanatory and lost nothing in translation into many European languages.

Siegfried Bettmann was the businessman and founder with Mauritz Shulte the engineer, both of whom moved to Coventry in 1888 with the intention of manufacturing their own machines. The reasoning for the move was to locate themselves in the centre of the cycle industry, as the skills of the Coventrian had long been recognised even in those early days.

In 1902 the Company produced their first motorcycle using a Minerva $2^1/4$ hp engine clipped to a cycle frame. It was not long before a Shulte-designed engine was used and 1905 saw the emergence of a totally in-house Triumph of 3 hp.

The new 3 hp soon gained a reputation for quality and reliability which was to be the hallmark of Triumph for the next eighty years. It would be no exaggeration to state that the Triumph Cycle Company's great faith in its product kept the motorcycle industry going in Coventry when contemporary firms making unreliable products were closing.

In 1913 a 600 cc vertical twin was experimented with but development did not continue due to the outbreak of war in 1914. This was the first known twin from this company. Later, in 1933, a Val Page-designed 633 cc vertical twin was produced but being rather old-fashioned in appearance it did not win public acclaim. Very soon after, the company fell into financial trouble like many others during the economic depression of the '30s. Indeed, so serious was the cash flow problem that bankruptcy and complete closure of the Triumph Cycle Company took place in 1936.

The Triumph pedal cycle side of the business was taken over by the Raleigh Cycle Company of Nottingham and the motor car side sold to The Standard Motor Company of Coventry. The remainder was purchased by John Sangster, the then owner of the Ariel car and motorcycle company of Birmingham, for a reputed figure of £30,000. It was said that he mortgaged everything he owned to raise the purchase sum, such was his desire and foresightedness to own Triumph. It did not take long for the newly formed Triumph Engineering Co Ltd to start production and Sangster sent over to Coventry one of his competent Ariel men in the form of Edward Turner to be Managing Director and Chief Designer. It proved a decision never to be regretted as from its inception the company went from strength to strength.

Very soon the youthful 35 year old Edward Turner had produced his own brand of vertical twin and it is fair to say it was to alter the course of motorcycling. It was to be copied over the next few years by a good many companies but none quite succeeded in getting that indiscernible quality that the Speed Twin possessed, good though they undoubtedly were.

Edward Turner was a capable rider and would always be on hand to test a 'new' model. Often he would catch the experimental department on the hop (we used to say he hid behind the door purposely) and demand the model be wheeled out so that he could leap astride and be off up the Birmingham road. In a brown leather coat and with a trilby hat pulled firmly down to his ears he would often be out for an hour or two appraising his latest project.

His rather impatient way often led to him riding off on the bike without the trade plates being attached (development bikes were never registered as this would cost money and Triumph were very good at looking after the pennies). I once remarked on this to my boss Frank Baker who retorted "Stop him, they wouldn't dare, he's Edward Turner!" and to our knowledge they (the police that is) never did or at least Edward Turner never let on if they did.

At the conclusion of his test ride if he was reasonably pleased the bike would be just parked outside the workshop. If, on the other hand, it really displeased him, it was not unknown for the bike to be deliberately dropped on his dismounting and he would storm up to his office leaving the bike where it lay.

In the cases where results did not live up to expectations, he would usually blame the design staff for not interpreting his instructions correctly but I feel this was always tongue in cheek. He had an uncanny knack of knowing which design to pursue and which to leave to gather the dust of the cellar to which the 'failures' were relegated.

One little saga, which always brings a smile, although nothing to do with the Speed Twin, was played out as follows. The development shop had produced without drawings a beautiful little swinging arm frame when Edward Turner was supporting the controversial spring hub. On spying the swinging arm frame he ordered his development foreman to put a saw through it and get rid of it. Although heartbroken, being a faithful employee he did as ordered and relegated it to the tip. About a fortnight later Edward Turner sent for the foreman saying 'Now then, go and get that frame and let's see what we can do". Foreman: 'But I've cut it up and got rid of it, sir, as you told me'. Edward Turner: "You idiot, when I said cut it up, I didn't mean cut it up!!' Exit foreman.

About two years later Triumph introduced their swinging arm frame. It was always reckoned that to get one of Edward Turner's designs changed, to confront him direct was folly, but if a reworked or redesigned part was left around for him to see, he would take the hint and a redesigned part would soon be on its way down from the drawing office.

Turner was a man of many talents – designer, financial director, chief salesman etc., so it is no surprise to learn that he organised a sales outlet in the USA through Bill Johnson in Pasadena.

When the first Speed Twins arrived in America they were an outstanding success. In no time at all they were winning on the speedway tracks and hill climbs, taking on the Indians and Harleys which generally were of twice the Triumph's cubic capacity.

It was not long before the Americans were looking for more power for the racing scene and Triumph responded with the tuned Speed Twin in the form of the Tiger 100. From here on the Speed Twin lost its pre-eminent place in the model range.

PART TWO

Development History

The Speed Twin, it was said and never strongly denied, owed its camshaft and engine configuration to that of the Riley Nine motor car, one of which Edward Turner had owned. The first public showing of the Speed Twin was at the Olympia Show in November 1937. It was acclaimed by the media as one of the outstanding models of the show and for once they were right as future years proved.

Its acceptance by a conservative motorcycling public was due no doubt to the fact that it did not look very different from the twin port single cylinder design with which everyone was familiar. The Speed Twin had all the benefits that a multi should have over a single such as smoother power impulses, greater flexibility and better low speed pulling. Other advantages were the capability of higher engine speeds and last but not least, much easier kick-starting.

As originally conceived and produced the Speed Twin did not generate a great deal more power than its single cylinder counterparts, producing approx. 28 bhp against the 24 bhp of a single, but due to its lighter revolving parts, it really zipped off the mark and felt much more responsive than the single.

Edward Turner's mania for lightness (every bought-in engine casting had to be weighed before and after machining and a report given to Edward Turner) was reflected in the fact that the Speed Twin weighed about 4 lbs less than its single cylinder counterpart yet cost only £5 more.

There is no doubt that the Speed Twin brought a mass produced multi to the pre-war motorcyclist at a price which, whilst not cheap, was within reach of a good many. That it was enjoyed by those purchasers will be seen in the various testimonies.

One of the first road test reports gave a glowing account of the performance. With a mean speed of 94 mph (rider prone) and with a tail wind, the best speed over the measured quarter mile was no less than 107 mph.

Minimum non-snatch speed was quoted as 12 mph in top gear with the ignition control lever in the fully retarded position. Overall average fuel consumption was given as 65 mpg which could be improved to 80 mpg if more careful use of the throttle was made.

It is a commonly-held belief in some quarters that the parallel or vertical twin was a blight on the industry with other manufacturers falling into line with Edward Turner's lead. Fact or fancy no one will ever be able fully to decide but certainly the vertical twin was there to stay and be almost universally adopted in the next fifty years.

Full testimony of Edward Turner's faith came in October 1938 when a supercharged

Speed Twin broke the Brooklands 500 cc lap record at 118.02 mph. A record which, incidentally, still stands.

Institutional Machines

From its introduction the Speed Twin found favour with the authorities for police and army use. The Metropolitan Police set the scene and police forces throughout the world followed their lead. In time the 650 cc 6T would take over the Speed Twin's role but not before the Speed Twin had made its mark and shown to the world the capability of an up-to-date modern motorcycle.

The Speed Twin found a ready market with many police forces; here 1938 models are on parade   9

Some of the total mileages covered by the Metropolitan Police and the Automobile Association were by motorcycle standards hardly creditable but were no less true. In 1946 "Torrens" wrote in *The Motor Cycle* "The Metropolitan Police have forty-two machines of which the average mileage is 98,000 and six have covered 150,000 whilst the largest single mileage is 161,000 and this last one will still do 75 mph."

The AA machines were always equipped with a sidecar and this of necessity was always fairly well laden but even these Speed Twins used to cover between 80,000 and 100,000 miles before they were put into the Triumph Service Department for overhaul.

The Triumph Engineering Company set a standard police specification but of course, various forces required additional and special items. The Metropolitan Police often required Speed Twins with both dynamo and alternator and previously laid down specifications were often adhered to long after the civilian model had changed. A perfect example of this is the use of a magneto on Metropolitan-built models in 1955, when coil ignition had been standard for two years.

On quite a number of Metropolitan Police models the dynamo was run faster by gearing up and this dyamo featured a slipping clutch in the drive to prevent damage during a kickback whilst starting.

IDENTIFICATION BY FRAME AND ENGINE NUMBER

Year	Engine number	Frame number	Dates built	Quantity	Remarks
1938	8-5T	TF or TH	Nov. 1937 Oct. 1938	–	
1939	9-5T	TF	Nov. 1938 Oct. 1939	–	
1940	40-5T	TF	Nov. 1939 –	– –	Possibly only small quantity made
1945	5-5T	TF	– Nov. 1945	–	
1946	6-5T	TF	Nov. 1945 Oct. 1946		
1947	7-5T	TF	Nov. 1946 Sept. 1947		
1948	8-5T 89214 8-5T 100688	TF 15001 TF 23714	4.9.1947 3.9.1948	6205	
1949	5T9 102603 5T9 113386	TF 25115 TF 33615	2.11.1948 6.10.1949	6850	End of TF series
1950	5T 1009N 5T 16100N	3618 16100N	18.10.1949 2.11.1950		End of N series
1951	5T 840NA 5T 15192NA	840NA 15192NA	20.11.1950 18.10.1951	3625	End of NA series
1952	5T 26096 5T 31901	26096 31901	24.3.1952 20.8.1952	1831	Common eng. & frame nos.
1953	5T 33868 5T 44774	33868 44774	18.10.1952 14.9.1953	3620	Commenced

1954	5T 45177 5T 55493	45177 55493	28.9.1953 7.7.1954	2305
1955	5T 55494 5T 70235	55494 70235	7.7.1954 9.8.1955	2760
1956	5T 71747 5T 82443	71747 82443	19.9.1955 27.6.1956	2187	Figures would reach six
1956	5T 0602 5T 02077	0602 02077	18.7.1956 25.9.1956		digits so new nos. commenced
1957	5T 02868 5T 010253	02868 010253	18.10.1956 20.8.1957	1349
1958	5T 011116 5T 020074	011116 020074	20.9.1957 28.8.1958	1083
1959	5T 023699 5T 023705	023699 023705	6.1.1959	6	Last pre- unit 5T
1959	5TA H 5785 5TA H 11035	H 5785 H 11035	25.9.1958 21.8.1959	2679	First unit- construction
1960	5TA H 11962 5TA H 18626	H 11962 H 18626	8.10.1959 1.9.1960	2207
1961	5TA H 19215 5TA H 24757	H 19215 H 24757	10.11.1960 22.8.1961	340
1962	5TA H 25904 5TA H 29727	H 25904 H 29729	26.9.1961 24.9.1962	375
1963	5TA H 30291 5TA H 32361	H 30291 H 32361	23.10.1962 1.8.1963	334
1964	5TA H 32918 5TA H 35986	H 32918 H 35986	13.10.1963 6.7.1964	530
1965	5TA H 37320 5TA H 39838	H 37320 H 39838	3.12.1964 1.6.1965	413
1966	5TA H 42227 5TA H 46431	H 42227 H 46431	8.9.1965 25.5.1966	590	Speed Twin production ended

PART THREE

The Early
Production Models

1938 Model 5T Speed Twin
Engine Prefix 8-5T

Engine

The vertical twin overhead valve gear was operated by high camshafts working in phosphor bronze bushes inside an aluminium crankcase.

The crankshaft consisted of a left and right crankweb bolted to a central flywheel by six high tensile bolts. The assembly was supported on two ball races, one each side.

Plain bearings were used for the big ends with white metal fused to the lower steel end caps whilst the upper half of the bearing was machined directly on to the hidiminium alloy con-rod.

The con-rods were of 'H' section and were fitted with a bronze bush in the small end to act as a bearing for the gudgeon pin.

Cylinder material was best grade cast iron as was the cylinder head. Bolted on to the cylinder head were two alloy rocker boxes housing the rockers and spindles giving full enclosure and lubrication to all moving parts.

The oil feed to the rockers was supplied from the timing cover via a small bore metal pipe, as was the pressure gauge mounted in the tank panel. A dry sump lubrication system was maintained by a twin piston plunger pump and the pressure controlled by a ball type release valve.

Ignition was supplied by a platform-mounted MN2 R03 anti-clockwise Lucas Magdyno situated to the rear of the cylinders and being gear driven off the inlet camshaft. The dynamo was a separate unit mounted on top of the magneto as was customary practice at that time. Ignition advance and retard control was cable-operated by a left-hand handlebar control lever.

An Amal Type 276 carburettor of $^{15}/_{16}$ in bore supplied the combustible mixture with the float chamber mounted on the right-hand side (this was due to the proximity of the dynamo). The choke was cable-operated from the right-hand handlebar lever. The twistgrip was of Triumph's own design and manufacture and was patented as such. It had a novel friction device consisting of a spring-loaded plunger contacting a finely serrated spool on the twistgrip drum. This gave a slightly notchy feel to the operation but was absolutely positive in staying at the given setting.

Gearbox

The gearbox was of Triumph's own design and manufacture, giving four speeds by well chosen ratios operating through a positive stop right-hand foot control.

Shafts and gears were of nickel chrome steel housed in a separate alloy casing; pivoting the gearbox case from the bottom gave provision for primary chain adjustment.

The mainshaft and high gear ran on ball journal races whilst the layshaft ran on a combination of cast iron and phosphor bronze bushes.

Primary transmission

The was by .305 in x $^1/2$ in chain from the engine sprocket to the clutch sprocket, housed in an oil bath of polished cast alloy. The shock absorber was incorporated in the engine sprocket/mainshaft assembly and consisted of a spring loaded face cam.

The clutch was a multi plate affair having alternate steel and corked plates with four pressure springs controlling the drive. Clutch operation was via a rod through the mainshaft to a lever on the right-hand side of the gearbox and then by cable to a left-hand mounted handlebar lever. A nice touch here was the small rubber cover over the cable nipple at the gearbox lever which was to be retained for many years.

Frame

The frame was a full cradle pattern using forged lugs into which were pinned and brazed tubes. It had a main frame consisting of tank and seat tubes with a tapering front downtube. Twin tubes running under the engine and gearbox were joined by a pair from the saddle nose at the rear wheel spindle.

A rear stand was incorporated, pivoting just below the rear wheel spindle. It was retained in the up position by a large spring anchored to the pillion footrest.

Suspension

Front forks were of the girder type having tapering tubes for strength. Springing was controlled by a single central spring and hand controlled friction dampers were built into the forward ends of the lower links. These could be adjusted from the saddle with the rider choosing the setting according to his needs. A central steering damper was controlled by a large Bakelite knob at the top of the steering tube.

Petrol tank

Of all welded construction and $3^1/4$ gallon capacity having a quick release hinged filler cap. Opening and closing was controlled by rotating a cross lever. The centre of the tank was deeply recessed to accommodate a switch panel, housing a pressure gauge, lighting switch, ammeter and an inspection lamp with extension lead.

Exhaust system

Two $1^3/4$ in down pipes, one on each side, terminated in parallel tubular silencers, all chrome plated.

Oil tank

This was of steel, all welded construction, having a capacity of six pints (Imp). It was fitted with a screwed aluminium filler cap.

Handlebars and controls

Of 1 in diameter tube swaged down at the right-hand end to $^{15}/16$ in to accommodate the Triumph twistgrip. Large rubber bushes were used on the handlebar mounting to insulate the rider from road shocks. The clutch and brake levers were of the solid forged type. Ignition and air control levers were of the round pattern, left and right handed. Horn and ignition cut out buttons were placed right and left handed respectively, with the dipper switch sited on the left.

Mudguards

These were of steel, both having a raised central band. The front guard had front and centre stays attached by rivets; the lower rear also also acting as a front stand. The rear guard was a two-part affair with the rear part being detachable just above the rear number plate top fixing to aid rear wheel removal. Two loop stays were riveted to the main part and one bolted to the detachable part. The main guard stays had threaded bosses attached to which were fitted two curved lifting handles.

Toolbox

A triangular toolbox was fitted between the rear chain stays on the right hand side. The lid was hinged on the lower edge and was retained in the closed position by a lever screw. Early toolboxes had a rubber weatherproof band which was later dispensed with.

Wheels

Of Triumph design and manufacture in WM2 size. The front was fitted with a 3.00 in x 20 in ribbed tyre and the rear fitted with a 3.50 in x 19 in Universal tyre. Dunlop tyres and tubes were fitted as standard equipment. Both brakes were of 7 in diameter, the front drum heavily ribbed to prevent distortion. Both drums were of best grade cast steel. The front anchor plate was of polished cast alloy whilst the rear was of pressed steel. Front brake operation was part cable and part rod whilst the rear was all rod. Adjustment for the rear was by a large round knurled nut and the front by a cable adjuster.

Seat

The seat was of De Luxe pattern, usually of Lycett or Terry manufacture. Long parallel chrome springs, adjustable for height, were used.

Electrical

The electrical system was 6 volt negative earth. Charging was by a Lucas E3HM dynamo via an automatic compensated voltage control box Type MCR 14. A Lucas D142F 8 in diameter chrome plate headlamp with fluted domed glass provided the front light whilst the rear was provided by a Lucas MT110.

The warning device was a Lucas HF934 Altette horn with chrome outer ring, attached to the left-hand seat spring bolt. A Lucas switch control RS 39/L1 was mounted in the petrol tank panel.

Speedometer

The 120 mph speedometer was mounted on top of the front forks being driven from the front wheel through a right-handle gearbox mounted in the front anchor plate. As an alternative a 180 kph speedometer was available at no extra cost.

Finish

All painted parts, with the exception of the following, were finished in amaranth red.

Number plates	Black
Pillion footrests	Black
Electric horn	Black
Brake return springs	Black
Rear stand return spring	Black
Instrument panel	Black
Voltage control box	Black – semi matt
Speedometer body	Black
Speedometer angle drive	Black – semi matt
Seat frame	Black

Mudguards – Amaranth red with gold line (approx. $1/8$ in wide) both sides of the raised centre band.
Petrol Tank – Amaranth red side and top panels on a chrome base. Twin gold lining approx. $3/32$ in outer followed by $3/32$ in chrome band with $5/32$ in inner line.
Wheel Rims – Amaranth red centre with approx. $1/8$ in gold lining on flat of rim.
Transfers –

Oil Tank		
Minimum Oil Level	–	Gilt
Drain Refill etc	–	Gilt
Recommended Lubricants	–	Gilt

Positions –

Drain and refill on front face of oil tank followed by Recommended Lubricants reading across the tank.

Minimum oil level – approx. halfway up the tank.

Rear Number Plate – Regd. Design – white/gilt.

Position – between bottom fixing bolts approx. length 3 in.

Many queries are raised regarding the Speed Twin amaranth red, the official Triumph version went thus:-

The amaranth are plants found mostly in tropical countries. They have a flower which is red in colour with a slight tinge of purple. A more common plant in British gardens is called *amaranth caudatus* by experts but *love lies bleeding* is good enough for most people. The flowers keep their colour even when picked and dried thus the excellent service given by the Triumph Speed Twin is reflected in its colour.

Most nuts and bolts were cadmium plated with only headlamp fixing bolts, rocker spindle dome nuts, fork spindle locknuts and handlebar fixing bolts being chrome plated.

Extras for 1938

Quickly detachable rear wheel	£2 0s 0d
Valanced front and rear mudguards	12s 6d
Prop stand assembly	10s 0d
Pillion footrest assembly	15s 0d
Pillion seat	12s 6d
Speedometer	£2 16s 0d
Carrier assembly	9s 3d
Air filter assembly	8s 0d

A 1938 Speed Twin which, with the aid of the artist's brush, has had such items as the HT leads, electrical cables and rear detachable mudguard joint removed

1938 Model 5T Speed Twin technical data

Technical Data
Engine

Bore	63mm	2.480 in
Stroke	80mm	3.15 in
Capacity	498cc	30.40 cu in
bhp (max)	28 at 6000 rpm	
Compression ratio	7.0:1	

Cylinder head

Material	Cast iron	
Valve seat angle	45°	
Valve seat width		
Inlet	0.050/0.060 in	
Exhaust	0.060/0.080 in	
Valve guide bore	0.4980/0.4985 in	

Valves

Stem diameter	
Inlet	0.3095/0.3100 in
Exhaust	0.3090/0.3095 in
Head diameter	$1^5/16$ in
Valve o/a length	Inlet and exhaust $3^{55}/64$ in

Valve guides

Material	Chilled cast iron
Bore diameter	0.312/0.313 in
Outside diameter	0.5005/0.5010 in
Length	
Inlet	$1^{31}/32$
Exhaust	$2^{11}/64$ in

Valve springs

Free length – nominal	
Inner	$1^5/8 \pm 1/16$ in
Outer	$2^1/32 \pm 1/16$ in

Fitted length

Inner	1.187 in
Outer	1.281 in

Cam follower

Foot radius	0.750 in
Stem diameter	0.3110/0.3115 in

Valve clearance – cold

Inlet and exhaust	0.001 in

Valve timing

IVO	21° BTDC	
IVC	75° ABDC	Nil clearance
EVO	75° BBDC	for checking
EVC	21° ATDC	

Push rods

Material	Tubular steel
Overall length	6.300/6.325 in

Rockers

Bore diameter	0.5002/0.5012 in
Spindle diameter	0.4990/0.4995 in

Camshafts and bearings

Journal diameter	
Left hand	0.8100/0.8105 in
Right hand	0.8730/0.8735 in
End float	0.013/0.020 in
Lobe height	1.047/1.055 in
Bush diameter	
Left hand bore	0.8125/0.8135 in
Right hand bore	0.874/0.875 in
Left hand outer	1/0010/1.0015 in
O/A length LH exhaust	0.932/0.942 in

LH inlet	0.932/0.942 in
RH inlet and exhaust	1.010/1.020 in

Cylinder barrel
Material	Cast iron
Cylinder bore diameter	2.4800/2.4805 in
Tappet guide bore	0.9985/0.9990 in
Max tolerable wear	0.007 in

Tappet block
Outer diameter	0.9995/1.000 in
Bore diameter	0.312/0.3125 in

Piston rings
Ring gap in cylinder bore
Compression ring	0.008/0.010 in
Scraper ring	0.010/0.012 in

Thickness (top to bottom face)
Compression ring	0.062 in
Scraper ring	0.124 in

Clearance in piston groove
Compression ring	0.002/0.003 in
Scraper ring	0.002/0.003 in

Pistons
Clearance in cylinder bore at maximum diameter (90° to gudgeon pin)	0.004 in
Crown height from gudgeon pin centre (7.0:1CR)	$1^3/_8$ in
Gudgeon pin diameter	0.6840 in

Connecting rods
Small end diameter	6.841/0.6843 in
Big end diameter	1.4375/1.4385 in
Side clearance (fitted)	0.012/0.030 in
Length between centres	6.499/6.501 in

Crankshaft
Crankpin diameter	1.4360/1.4365 in
Main bearing journal diameter	
Drive side	1.1247/1.1250 in
Timing side	0.9997/1.0000 in
Crankshaft end float	0.003/0.017 in
Oil feed journal diameter	0.622/0.623 in
Balance factor	52%

Crankshaft bearings
Drive side	1.125 x 2.812 x 0.812 in
Timing side	1.00 x 2.50 x 0.750 in
Oil feed bush	0.6245/0.6255 in
Bearing	Ball t/s and d/s

Oil pump
Feed plunger diameter	0.3121/0.3125 in
Scavenge plunger diameter	0.4371/0.4374 in

Feed bore	0.31225/0.31275 in
Scavenge bore	0.43725/0.43775 in

Carburettor

Type	276/132 LH
Bore	$^{15}/_{16}$ in
Main jet	140
Needle jet	.107
Needle	No. 6
Needle position	3
Throttle valve	6/3
Float chamber	64/195

Ignition

Magdyno	Lucas
Timing	37° or $^3/_8$ in BTDC fully adv.
Points gap	0.012 in
Spark plug	KLG 831
Plug gap	0.018 in
Thread size	14 mm
Reach	$^1/_2$ in

Clutch

Corked plates	4
Plain plates	5
Pressure springs	4
Spring free length	$1^1/_2$ in
Bearing rollers	20
Roller size	
Diameter	0.2495/0.250 in
Length	0.231/0.236 in
Hub bearing diameter	1.3733/1.3743 in
Sprocket bore diameter	1.8745/1.8755 in
Clutch rod diameter	$^7/_{32}$ in
Clutch rod o/a length	$11^3/_4$ in (Nominal)

Kickstart mechanism

Case bore diameter LH	0.6245/0.6255 in
Bush bore diameter RH	0.751/0.752 in
K/S spindle diameter RH	0.748/0.749 in
K/S spindle diameter LH	0.6215/0.6225 in
Ratchet sleeve o/d	0.8747/0.8752 in
Ratchet spring free length	$^1/_2$ in

Gearchange mechanism

Quadrant plunger	
Outer diameter	0.4315/0.4320 in
Plunger bore	0.4325/0.4330 in
Plunger spring	
No. of coils	12
Free length	$1^1/_4$ in

Footchange spindle

Diameter LH	0.6215/0.6235 in
Diameter RH	0.747/0.749 in
Bush LH bore diameter	0.6245/0.6255 in
Bush LH outer diameter	0.8755/0.8765 in

Bush RH bore diameter   0.7495/0.7505 in
Bush RH outer diameter   0.8755/0.8765 in

Quadrant springs
Free length $1^3/4$ in
No. of coils   12

Camplate plunger
Plunger diameter   0.436/0.4365 in
Housing bore   0.4375/0.438 in
Spring length $2^1/2$ in
No. of coils   19

Mainshaft
Bearing LH $1^1/4$ x $2^1/2$ x $5/8$ in ball
Bearing RH $3/4$ x $1^7/8$ x $9/16$ in ball
Mainshaft diameter LH   0.8120/0.8125 in
Mainshaft sleeve bush
    Inside diameter   0.8135/0.8145 in
    Outer diameter   0.909/0.910 in
    O/A length $2^1/4$ in

Layshaft
Bearing diameter LH/RH   0.560/0.5605 in
Bush bore diameter LH/RH   0.562/0.563 in
Bush outside diameter LH/RH   0.688/0.689 in
Layshaft sleeve bush $1^3/8$ in x 0.7498/0.7505 in
Layshaft lowgear bush
    Inside diameter   0.7493/0.7500 in
    Outside diameter   0.8444/0.8454 in

Number of teeth on pinions

Layshaft		Mainshaft
19	4th	25
21	3rd	23
25	2nd	19
29	1st	15

Sprockets

	Solo	Sidecar
Engine	22	19
Clutch	43	43
Gearbox	18	18
Rear wheel	46	46

Gear ratios – internal

4th	1.00
3rd	1.20
2nd	1.73
1st	2.54

Overall ratios

	Solo	Sidecar
4th	5.00	5.8
3rd	6.00	6.95
2nd	8.65	10.00
1st	12.7	14.70

rpm at 10 mph top gear 646

Chains

Primary	$5/16$ in x $1/2$ in 78 link solo
	$5/16$ in x $1/2$ in x 77 link sidecar
Secondary	$3/8$ in x $5/8$ in x 92 link

Wheels

Rims
Front	WM2 x 20 in
Rear	WM2 x 19 in

Tyres
Front	3.25 in x 20 in ribbed
Rear	3.50 in x 19 in Universal

Brakes

Diameter	7 in
Width	$1^1/8$ in

Bearings

Front – taper roller	$7/16$ in x $1^7/16$ in x $11/16$ in x $7/16$ in outer
Rear – taper roller	$9/16$ in x $1^3/4$ in x $13/16$ in x $9/16$ in outer

Spokes front	Rear
RH 10 off 9G 80° x $9^1/16$ in	RH 10 off 9G 76° x 9 in
RH 10 off 9G 97° x $9^1/16$ in	RH 10 off 9G 100° x 9 in
LH 10 off 9G 80° x $9^3/8$ in	LH 10 off 9G 76° x $8^3/4$ in
LH 10 off 9G 97° x $9^3/8$ in	LH 10 off 9G 100° x $8^3/4$ in

Wheel offset

Front – dimension from drum fixing face to centre of rim 1 in
Rear – dimension from outside edge of sprocket to centre of rim $3^5/32$ in

Frame

Steering head bearings
Top	22 off $3/16$ in ball
Bottom	20 off $1/4$ in ball

Dimensions

Wheelbase	54 in
Overall length	84 in
Overall width	$28^1/2$ in
Seat height	$29^1/2$ in adjustable
Weight dry	355 lb
Ground clearance	6 in

Lubrication

Engine – summer	SAE 50
winter	SAE 30
Gearbox	EP 80/90
Primary chaincase	SAE 20
Grease	Castrol LM

Capacities

Fuel tank	$3^1/4$ Imp gal.
Oil tank	6 pint
Gear box	$3/4$ pint EP 90
Primary case	$1/4$ pint SAE 20

Electrical

Dynamo	E3HM-L-0 40 watt
Voltage regulator	MCR-L-4
Voltage	6V
Earth	Negative
Bulb main	6V 24/30W
Bulb, pilot	6V 3W
Bulb, speedometer	6V 2.5W
Bulb, tail	6V 3W
Bulb, inspection	6V 3W
Battery	Lucas 6V 12 ampere – hour

Torque settings

Con-rod nuts	28 lb. ft.
Flywheel nuts	12 lb. ft.
Cylinder head bolts	18 lb. ft.
Camshaft pinion nuts	50 lb. ft.
Crankshaft pinion nut	50 lb. ft.
Engine sprocket nut	80 lb. ft.
Oil release valve	15 lb. ft.
Clutch shaft nut	50 lb. ft.
Kickstart ratchet nut	30 lb. ft.
Gearbox sprocket nut	80 lb. ft.

Left-hand threads

Camshaft pinion nuts

NEW TRIUMPH DESCRIBED

An Interesting o.h.v. Vertical Twin Engine

BECAUSE it is well known that Mr. Edward Turner, managing director of the Triumph Engineering Co., Ltd., was the designer of that very ingenious and unconventional engine, the Ariel Square Four, it has been freely supposed that the new Triumph "multi" also would have four cylinders arranged in some novel but practical way. However, Mr. Turner, as those who know him well are quite aware, has anything but a single-track mind and in actual fact this interesting Triumph newcomer has two cylinders and a very simple general arrangement.

Nevertheless it does contain ingenious and unusual features and it would be highly inaccurate to think of this new model as simply a later and smaller edition of the old 650 c.c. twin. In fact none of the parts is the same as those of the earlier engine.

Compact and Light.

Up to a point it is true there is similarity. The two cylinders are vertical in one casting and the crankshaft lies across the machine. Moreover, both pistons rise and fall together. There the likeness ends.

The new engine is complete in itself and is not combined with a gearbox. It fits into a frame which is for most practical purposes the same as that of the Tiger "90" and, apart from the fact that the twin engine is a trifle lighter, the weight distribution of these two motorcycles is identical.

It has already been mentioned that the cylinders are vertical and are formed in a single casting. This is mounted on a crankcase of conventional style which is only slightly broader than that of a single. It carries on two bearings as usual a crankshaft which consists of three parts.

At the centre is a small flywheel with integral balance weights. Spigoted into each side of this is a piece which comprises a short shaft, a web, a crankpin and a circular flange which fits into the flywheel spigot and is held to it by bolts passing through the flywheel and the two flanges.

When assembled the two crankpins are in line, so that the firing intervals are evenly spaced. Because the two pistons move together and not in opposite directions, the balance is of precisely the same kind as a single. The forces involved, however, are somewhat smaller than in a single of the same capacity because the stroke is so much shorter.

Unusual Big-ends.

Actually the stroke is 80 mm. and the bores measure 63 mm., giving a total swept volume of 498 c.c. The compression ratio is about 7 to 1, a moderate figure for cylinders of this size, but the power developed is stated to be 29 b.h.p. at 6,000 r.p.m.

From what has been said of the crankshaft, students of design will have realized that rollers are not used for the big ends. Actually these are plain bearings, but not of quite the usual type. It should be explained that each connecting rod is an RR 56 Hiduminium forging. This material has excellent bearing qualities, but it lacks one feature of white metal. In an emergency such as the failure, temporary or otherwise, of the oil supply, white metal will fuse. This automatically provides additional clearance so that the bearing and shaft will not seize together to the detriment of both.

From these facts arises the big-end bearing design of this new Triumph twin. To take full advantage of the light Hiduminium rod it is arranged to bear directly on the steel crankpin. The bearing cap to complete the circle embracing the crank is, however, a steel forging lined with white metal. In this way the advantages of both metals are retained, together with a strong and rigid bearing cap.

No detailed description of the pistons is necessary because they are simple full-skirted affairs of well-tried type. Nor is there any novelty in the timing gear which consists of five wheels. A small one is mounted on the crankshaft and it drives an idler wheel above it. This in turn drives two half-speed gears arranged one on each side and slightly higher up.

The Cam Arrangement.

Each of these is mounted on a camshaft and the rear one meshes with the fifth gear which is attached to the shaft of a Lucas Magdyno placed behind the cylinders. Returning to the camshafts which are located one at the back and one at the front of the crankcase near its top, each shaft runs rather more than half-way across the engine and is mounted in two plain bearings.

On each shaft there are two cams very close together astride the centre line of the engine. The rear camshaft operates the inlet valves and the front one the exhausts, but the cam contours are identical in both cases and the two camshafts are interchangeable.

Immediately above each pair of cams is a phosphor-bronze block which carries

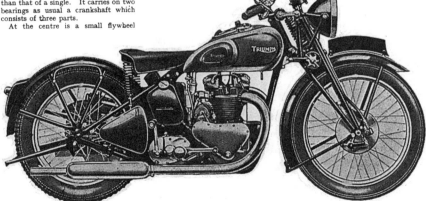

The new Triumph vertical twin is a remarkably good-looking machine. It has none of the bulkiness usually associated with "multis" and the engine actually weighs slightly less than a standard "90."

(above & pages 22, 23) **A first full description of the new Triumph twin**

21

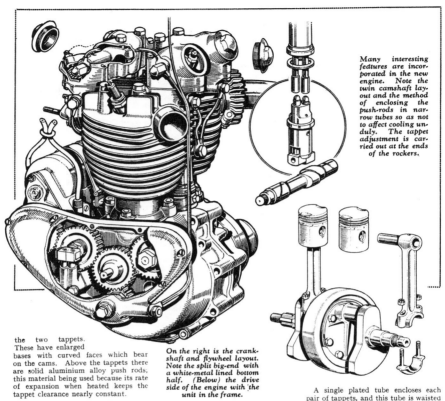

Many interesting features are incorporated in the new engine. Note the twin camshaft layout and the method of enclosing the push-rods in narrow tubes so as not to affect cooling unduly. The tappet adjustment is carried out at the ends of the rockers.

the two tappets. These have enlarged bases with curved faces which bear on the cams. Above the tappets there are solid aluminium alloy push rods; this material being used because its rate of expansion when heated keeps the tappet clearance nearly constant.

On the right is the crankshaft and flywheel layout. Note the split big-end with a white-metal lined bottom half. (Below) the drive side of the engine with the unit in the frame.

A single plated tube encloses each pair of tappets, and this tube is waisted or reduced in diameter for most of its length so that it causes very little obstruction to the flow of air between the cylinders which, although in one casting, are spaced sufficiently far apart to have fins between them.

The Valve-gear.

Each tube is provided with good oil-tight joints at both ends, and it need never be disturbed except when decarbonizing. Adjustment of tappet clearances is made at the push-rod end of each overhead rocker, there being a conventional lock-nut and set screw with a ball-end bearing in the cupped steel top of the push rod.

Both cylinder heads are formed in a single casting and the combustion spaces are hemispherical. The valves are arranged at a wide angle, the exhausts sloping forward, of course, and the inlets backward. Two light alloy castings mounted, one across the front and one across the back of the cylinder-head casting, enclose the valve stems and springs. They also carry the overhead rockers, and opposite each point of adjustment there is a screwed cap with a hexagon. The latit easy to tighten the cap so as to avoid oil leaks and, of course, removal of the cap makes tappet adjustment very simple.

Each cylinder has a single exhaust port from which a nicely curved pipe leads back to a cylindrical silencer by the chain stays, the appearance being very much that of an ordinary two-port engine. The inlet ports also are separate and are connected by a small Y-piece to a slightly down-draught Amal carburetter.

Lubrication.

Finally, so far as the engine is concerned, a word about the lubrication system. In the lower part of the timing case there is a double plunger pump of the usual Triumph pattern driven by an eccentric pin and sliding block. This pump is rather larger than its predecessor, and it delivers oil at a pressure of some 50 lb. per sq. inch.

Oil is fed to the big-end bearings through passages drilled in the crank-shaft. A separate supply is taken by an external pipe to the two rocker boxes and is fed direct to the rocker bearings through the fixed spindles. The surplus is carried by short pipes into the push-rod tubes and thus lubricates the tappets and cams.

This interesting and very practical engine is mounted in a machine which in all other respects resembles the Triumph Tiger "90" 500 c.c. single. In spite of its extra exhaust pipe and silencer, the complete twin motorcycle weighs a trifle less than the single, but in other respects they are alike, and even in appearance the twin might easily be mistaken for a two-port single.

Solo gear ratios are 5.0, 6.0, 8.65 and 12.7 to 1, the sidecar ratios being 5.8, 6.95, 10.0 and 14.7 to 1. Both tyres

The off side of the new Triumph twin unit. The two hexagon-headed caps give easy access to the valve tappet adjustment; below them will be noticed the pipes which drain surplus oil from the rocker box into the push-rod tube. Incidentally, how unusual is the appearance of an o.h.v. engine's timing side without push-rods.

are 26 ins. by 3.25 ins. The wheel-base measures 54 ins., and the overall length is 84 ins.

This is undoubtedly an interesting machine, but it is much more than that. From the earliest drawing-board stage trouble has been notably absent, we understand, and one of the experimental models with sidecar attached has covered 10,000 miles on the road in all weather and in a comparatively short time. Speeds of 90 m.p.h. solo are spoken of.

At an early date we shall publish a full road test report, but already it seems clear that an outstanding machine has been added to the list of British motorcycles.

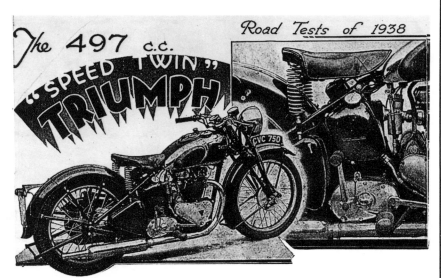

The 497 c.c. "SPEED TWIN" TRIUMPH

Road Tests of 1938

So compact and neat is the engine of the "Speed Twin" that the machine can easily be mistaken for a "single." The frame and other components are similar to those used for the single-cylinder Triumph models

The accessibility of the Triumph is clearly shown in this close-up of the engine. The neatly arranged oil leads and simple induction manifold are typical of the thoroughness of the design

NO one needs reminding that the new vertical-twin Triumph was one of the outstanding machines at the Earls Court Motor Cycle Show. Nor is it necessary to recapitulate the many interesting features of its design, beyond, perhaps, mentioning the high-camshaft mountings, the light-alloy connecting rods, the plain big-end bearings and the pressure-feed lubrication system.

The engine, which looks at first glance a single-cylinder, is so compact that it is housed without alteration of chain-line in the normal Triumph "Tiger 90" frame. Nor is there any need to add that it was with considerable anticipation that one of these machines was taken over for road test! It may be said right away that the machine submitted for test amply fulfilled the high claims made by its makers; its all-round performance was surprising.

No decompressor is fitted to the "Speed Twin" Triumph and none was found necessary, for the engine would start immediately under all conditions. When the engine was cold it was necessary to flood the carburettor and a fairly hearty kick was required. At all other times a gentle dig on the kick-starter would set the engine ticking over. With the ignition retarded the slow running was excellent and could be relied upon in traffic. At one period during the test the slow running disappeared, but this was quickly traced to a loose adjuster in the throttle cable.

Whether the engine was idling or on larger throttle openings, mechanical noise was very slight. At very low speeds a certain amount of mechanical noise could be heard, but this was no greater than that of a good 500 c.c. single at similar speeds. Once the machine was on the move all traces of mechanical sound disappeared and at high speeds the engine could not be heard even when the rider turned his head out of the air stream.

At no time was the exhaust noise objectionable; at low road speeds the exhaust was almost inaudible, while at speeds of 60 m.p.h. and over it developed into a pleasant low zoom.

So much then for general features of the machine. It is in the engine's performance that the real delight of the "Speed Twin" lies. So versatile did the engine

		PERFORMANCE DATA.		
Gear.		Maximum Speeds.	Acceleration.	
			15-30 m.p.h.	20-50 m.p.h.
First (12.7)	...	46 m.p.h.	2¼ secs.	—
Second (8.65)	...	62 m.p.h.	3¼ secs.	6 secs.
Third (6.0)	...	80 m.p.h.	5 secs.	8¼ secs.
Top (5.0)	...	93.75 m.p.h.	7 secs.	11¼ secs.

Speed attained over ¼ mile through gears from standing start : 74 m.p.h.
Braking from 30 m.p.h. in top gear : 30 feet.
Fuel consumption at a maintained 40 m.p.h. : 82.2 m.p.g.
Minimum non-snatch speed in top gear : 12 m.p.h.

(above & pages 25, 26) **One of the first road test reports**

24

Models

The push-rod tubes are carried in the vees formed by the cylinders. Access to the tappets is gained by removing the screwed caps on the rocker boxes. The pipes leading from the rocker gear to the push-rod tubes are oil drains

prove that the machine was equally at home in the thickest traffic or on the fastest main road. In traffic it would trickle along perfectly happily at 20 m.p.h. in top gear, and would accelerate rapidly and smoothly from this speed. If need be, the engine, with the ignition retarded, could be throttled down to 12 m.p.h. in top gear without any transmission snatch. If the gears were used, acceleration well above average was available. To accelerate from 15 to 30 m.p.h. in bottom gear, for example, took only $2\frac{2}{5}$ seconds. In second gear, the one normally used for hurried acceleration, less than four seconds was required. Even in top gear the time taken was only seven seconds.

Similarly on the open road, the acceleration was excellent, as a glance at the figures in the table shows.

On the Open Road

Much of the joy in driving the model comes, however, from the delightful way the machine will zoom from 30 m.p.h. to 60, 70 or 80 m.p.h. at the will of the rider without his having to touch any control other than the twist-grip. Some idea of the model's performance when the gears are used can be obtained from the fact that 74 m.p.h. was reached in a quarter of a mile from a standing start.

On the open road the machine was utterly delightful. Ample power for all conditions was always available at a turn of the twist-grip, and the lack of noise when the machine was cruising in the seventies was almost uncanny. Main road hills were taken in the model's stride with just a little more throttle opening, and even on very steep hills or on hills with sharp bends which necessitated a change down, the acceleration available

would rapidly bring the machine back to a high cruising speed. Thus it was found that large mileages were tucked into the hour without the rider consciously hurrying, and long runs were accomplished with less mental effort than usual.

Even when the performance figures already quoted are borne in mind, the sheer maximum speed of the machine is surprising. The timed tests were carried out on a day when there was a fair breeze blowing. With the rider clad in a single-piece "International" suit and lying well down along the tank (sitting on the mudguard, there being no pillion seat) the mean speed of four runs, two with and two against the wind, was 93.75 m.p.h.

The best timed run with the wind behind gave a speed over the quarter-mile of 107 m.p.h.—truly an

---

SPECIFICATION

TYPE : "Speed Twin" model.

ENGINE : 63 × 80 mm. (497 c.c.) vertical twin-cylinder o.h.v. Triumph with totally enclosed valve gear and dry-sump lubrication.

CARBURETTOR : Amal with special Triumph twist-grip control.

GEAR BOX : Triumph four-speed with enclosed foot change.

TRANSMISSION : Chain with primary oil bath and double rear chain guard.

IGNITION : Lucas Magdyno.

LIGHTING : Lucas 6-volt with voltage control and tank-top switch panel.

FUEL CAPACITY : 3¼ gals.

TYRES : Dunlop, 3.00—20 ribbed front ; 3.50—19 "Universal" rear.

GROUND CLEARANCE : 5in.

WEIGHT : 365 lb. fully equipped.

PRICE : £77 15s., with full electrical equipment and 120 m.p.h. illuminated speedometer.

MAKERS : Triumph Engineering Co. Ltd., Coventry.

amazing figure for a fully equipped five-hundred. Moreover, so steady was the model at this speed that the rider found it difficult to realise that the machine was travelling so quickly. Naturally, the steering damper was tightened down for the tests of maximum speed, but at no other time was it used or found necessary.

The steering and handling of the machine on the road are excellent. The only criticism was that the rear wheel had a tendency to hop on uneven surfaces. Cornering and general manœuvrability proved to be of a very high order, and the model, with its low centre of gravity, felt more like a two-fifty than a five-hundred from the point of view of ease of handling.

It is extremely fortunate that the Triumph *is* so well-mannered, for owing to the smoothness and silence of the engine there was a distinct tendency for the rider to take corners at higher speeds than usual, but even on corners rounded at really high speeds the Triumph was perfectly steady and safe.

A high degree of balance has been achieved with the Triumph, and apart from a slight period around 60 m.p.h. in top gear the engine is perfectly smooth and sweet. It may even be said that the period is only noticeable because of the exceptional smoothness of the engine at all other speeds, and at no time was the vibration sufficient to cause any discomfort.

Well Chosen Ratios

The Triumph four-speed gear box was delightfully quiet on all gears. The clutch was free from drag and the gear change was light and positive.

The gear ratios are well chosen and the maximum speeds reached by the machine in the indirect gears were : Third (6 to 1), 80 m.p.h. ; second (8.65 to 1), 62 m.p.h. ; and bottom (12.7 to 1), 46 m.p.h. With regard to the figures for bottom and second gear, it should be mentioned that the engine at these speeds was being grossly over-revved.

For normal speeds and for persons of normal height

the riding position is good. The controls are well placed and the brake and gear lever pedals are in convenient positions. For a tall rider, however, the saddle is somewhat too near the handlebars. With the saddle moved back a little way it is probable that the tendency towards rear-wheel hop at high speeds would be overcome ; at the same time the riding position would be improved. These remarks apply only to fast road work. At normal speeds the riding position is comfortable and the supple saddle and wide range of movement of the front forks successfully smooth out road shocks.

The new Triumph twist-grip with internal ratchet is pleasant in use, and all feeling of the ratchet is lost when the machine is on the road, yet the grip remains positive in action. On the model tested there was a tendency for the throttle to close if the hand was removed from the grip at high speeds.

Clean and Smart

As is to be expected with a machine of such a high general standard as the Triumph, the brakes proved to be first class. Both were extremely powerful and smooth, and applied together they would bring the model to rest from 30 m.p.h. in a fraction less than 30ft.

In economy the Triumph also scored, for at a maintained speed of 40 m.p.h. the petrol consumption was 82 m.p.g. A small trouble that occurred in the course of the test was the fracture of the angle bracket used for the attachment of the front end of the fuel tank.

Finally, mention must be made of the machine's appearance. The standard finish is amaranth red. It is a plum colour and looks extremely smart in conjunction with the chromium plating on other parts of the machine. At the conclusion of the test, which included hundreds of miles of really hard driving, the Triumph was as clean and smart as at the beginning, and apart from a very slight seep of oil from the rear end of the primary chain case, not a spot of oil had leaked from any of the joints of the power unit.

Sir Malcolm Campbell's Opinion

Sir Malcolm Campbell, three Times Holder of World's Land Speed Record.

27 Nov 1939

       In my opinion, the Triumph Speed Twin has no equal. It is a machine eminently suitable for all purposes, is an extremely sound engineering job, and the workmanship is superb.

       I acquired my first Triumph motor cycle in 1908, and was never without one until the outbreak of the Great War in 1914. I now own a Triumph Speed Twin, and a Tiger 100, and so long as I indulge in this pastime I shall continue to use the machines made by this eminent firm.

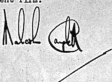

Praise from Sir Malcolm Campbell

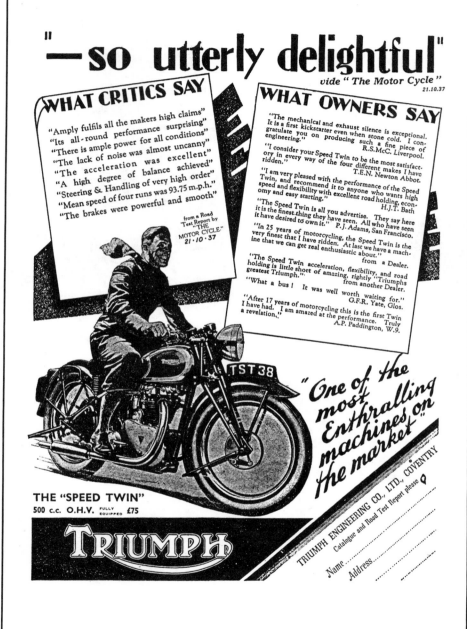

"— so utterly delightful"

vide "The Motor Cycle"
21.10.37

WHAT CRITICS SAY

"Amply fulfils all the makers high claims"
"Its all-round performance surprising"
"There is ample power for all conditions"
"The lack of noise was almost uncanny"
"The acceleration was excellent"
"A high degree of balance achieved"
"Steering & Handling of very high order"
"Mean speed of four runs was 93.75 m.p.h."
"The brakes were powerful and smooth"

from a Road
Test Report by
"THE
MOTOR CYCLE."
21·10·37

WHAT OWNERS SAY

"The mechanical and exhaust silence is exceptional.
It is a first kickstarter even when stone cold. I congratulate you on producing such a fine piece of engineering."
R.S.McC. Liverpool.

"I consider your Speed Twin to be the most satisfactory in every way of the four different makes I have ridden."
T.E.N. Newton Abbot.

"I am very pleased with the performance of the Speed Twin, and recommend it to anyone who wants high speed and flexibility with excellent road holding, economy and easy starting."
H.J.T. Bath

"The Speed Twin is all you advertise. They say here it is the finest thing they have seen. All who have seen it have desired to own it."
P.J. Adams, San Francisco.

"In 25 years of motorcycling, the Speed Twin is the very finest that I have ridden. At last we have a machine that we can get real enthusiasts about."
from a Dealer.

"The Speed Twin acceleration, flexibility, and road holding is little short of amazing, rightly "Triumphs greatest Triumph.""
from another Dealer.

"What a bus! It was well worth waiting for."
G.F.R. Yate, Glos.

"After 17 years of motorcycling this is the first Twin I have had. I am amazed at the performance. Truly a revelation."
A.P. Paddington, W.9.

"One of the most Enthralling machines on the market"

THE "SPEED TWIN"
500 c.c. O.H.V. FULLY EQUIPPED £75

TST 38

TRIUMPH

TRIUMPH ENGINEERING CO., LTD., COVENTRY
Catalogue and Road Test Report please

Name..................
Address................

Unstinted praise from the buyers who rode them

Records!

NON-ENGINE STOP RECORD

UNDER A.C.U. OBSERVATION IN SOUTH AUSTRALIA.

A TRIUMPH motor cycle with sidecar attached embarked on an ambitious non-engine stop test early in 1938. It proved to be the longest test of its type ever recorded. Under Australian colonial conditions 9261 miles were covered in

13 Days and 13 Nights

the engine running continuously. Wheel stops were made for refuelling and refreshments only —a striking demonstration of the reliability and stamina which is built into every Triumph and a tribute to the riders, S. Goodsell and R. Aldridge. After 9261 miles had been covered the sparking plug gap had widened and refused to function otherwise, as mentioned in the Australian report, the engine would have continued to run.

BROOKLANDS

350 c.c. LAP RECORD

E ARLY in 1939 this record was broken by a 343 c.c. O.H.V. Single Cylinder Triumph at a speed of

105.97 m.p.h.

BROOKLANDS

FASTEST 250 c.c. LAP

S ECURED on a 249 c.c. O.H.V. Single Cylinder Triumph at a speed of

97 m.p.h.

In a 3-Lap Outer Circuit All-Comers' Race the 249 c.c. Triumph achieved an average speed of 92.9 m.p.h. 250, 350 and 500 c.c. Triumph motor cycles, although not built for racing purposes have, with their standard but individually tested engines, secured these outstanding speed records during the past twenty-two months.

12 & 24-HOUR RECORDS BROKEN

UNDER A.C.U. OBSERVATION IN SOUTH AUSTRALIA.

12-Hour Record. The existing record of 700 miles was broken in 1938 by Les Friedricks on a standard Triumph "Speed Twin". He covered 806 miles at an average speed of 70 m.p.h. (actual running time), breaking the previous record by 106 miles.

24-Hour Record. Les Friedricks, again on a standard Triumph Twin, broke this record by 196 miles. With the exception of stops for refuelling and refreshments he rode

Twice round the Clock

on a 12½ mile circuit beset by rocks, soft going and sharp ¼-mile turns at every 6 miles. His average speed, including stops, was 62.5 m.p.h. and speeds up to 85 m.p.h. on the straights were indulged in—a magnificent performance by man and machine.

BROOKLANDS

500 c.c. LAP RECORD BROKEN at 118.02 m.p.h.

BY A PRIVATE OWNER ON A STANDARD TRIUMPH "SPEED TWIN".

O NE of the most important motor cycle records in the calendar was broken at Brooklands in October, 1938, when Mr. I. B. Wicksteed, riding a Triumph "Speed Twin" to which he had fitted a supercharger, lapped Brooklands outer circuit in 1 min. 24.8 secs., **averaging 118.02 m.p.h. in heavy rain.** Previous record held by a 500 c.c. machine was at a speed of 116.63 m.p.h. It should be pointed out that the concrete track was treacherously slippery and a high wind from the south-west was against Wicksteed when he put up this astonishing performance and he came within 5 m.p.h. of the unlimited record made by the late Mr. E. C. Ferniough on a machine of nearly double the capacity.

Photographs by "The Motor Cycle".

Mr. I. B. Wicksteed at the start of his record-breaking effort and at speed on the track.

Records broken

1939 Model 5T Speed Twin
Engine Prefix 9-5T
Alterations for 1939

Valve timing

IVO	26°	BTDC
IVC	69°	ABDC
EVO	61°	BBDC
EVC	35°	ATDC

Cylinder barrel
The six stud fixing at the cylinder/crankcase joint was strengthened by a change to eight stud fixing, following T100 practice.

Primary chaincase
The alloy oil bath chaincase had added provision for rear chain lubrication. This took the form of a tapering screw retained by a coil spring, allowing oil through and down a small trough which in theory was supposed to deposit oil on the chain. It did, but it also lubricated many a girl friend's silk stocking! Most owners screwed the adjuster fully home and used a good old fashioned oil can.

Lubrication
Rocker oil feed pressure was reduced by the introduction of a restrictor. This took the form of a coarse threaded stud screwed into a threaded tube. Oil supply was regulated by altering the depth of the stud in the tube as oil had to pass around the outside of the stud thread i.e. the more thread in the tube the less oil and vice versa.

Shock Absorber
The engine shaft shock absorber cam contour was changed to provide smoother operation.

Petrol Tank
The tank badges were changed to diecast in relief with a red background – these replaced the embossed type.

Front Number Plate
A chrome diecast bead was added around the front number plate.

Handlebars
The handlebars were reduced in width and given a more rearward angle, to provide a better riding position.

Speedometer
The speedometer was reworked to show engine revolutions in each gear as well as miles per hour.

Headlamp
The domed headlamp glass of '38 was replaced by one that was fluted and flat.

Price
The price was reduced to £74. 0s. 0d.

Extras

120 mph speedometer	£2 15s 0d
120 mph speedometer 5″ dial	£5 5s 0d
Rear stop light	6s 0d
Pillion footrests	7s 6d
Pillion seat	12s 6d
Prop stand	10s 0d
Quickly detachable rear wheel	£2 0s 0d
Valanced mudguards	12s 6d

Unique Features

Triumph motor cycles, despite their handsome appearance and acknowledged general excellence, may appear in many respects to be largely orthodox in design. They incorporate, however, so large a number of genuinely exclusive features that they are in a class of their own. A few of these features are illustrated here.

(1) RIBBED BRAKE DRUM:

Combining rigidity with long life for the brake lining and rapid heat dissipation under prolonged use, this drum is made from an alloy which has been selected after extensive tests as the most suitable. Triumph brakes are almost indestructible and withstand the hardest use with the minimum of adjustment.

(2) PETROL TANK—TIGER '100' (Registered Design No. 830,475). With a large capacity (four gallons) and a shapely streamlined contour, this tank carries knee grips in recessed panels with the result that a comfortable riding position is combined with correct weight distribution and a most imposing appearance. The instrument panel of moulded construction carries an external light which gives really adequate illumination and may be used as an inspection lamp.

(3) SILENCERS—TIGER '100'

The readily detachable tail-piece carries with it all the baffles and after its removal leaves the open megaphone portion suitable for racing.

(4) FRONT NUMBERPLATE :

With neat chromium plated beading and motif, this new numberplate is entirely free from sharp edges and corners, is strong and sets off the appearance of the front end of the machine.

(5) REAR NUMBERPLATE : (Registered Design No. 820869). Of a stream-lined shape which blends with the lines of the machine this numberplate is very strong and provides a neat and well protected mounting for the rear lamp.

(6) GEARBOX

The Triumph gearbox with its patented all-enclosed footchange and clutch operating mechanism is, in proportion to its load carrying capacity, the most compact on the market.

First class design, workmanship, and materials ensure a high standard of silence and oil-tightness. Externally, it is shapely and free from awkward angles and places for lodgement of dirt.

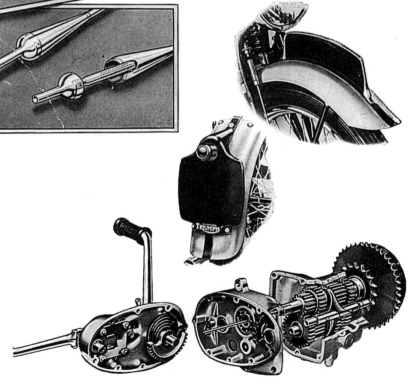

1939 features

THE MAUDES TROPHY

A Speed Twin in company with a Tiger 100 achieved a wonderful demonstration of reliability and for this the company was awarded the Maudes Trophy. Pre-war this prize was highly coveted and any manufacturer lucky enough to have it awarded could make good use of the publicity which would follow.

The Maudes Trophy originated when Mr. George Pettyt, proprietor of Maudes Motor Mart, decided in 1923 that an event was needed to publicise the capabilities of the touring motorcycle. He presented a trophy to be awarded each year to the manufacturer whose product made the best meritorious performance in an ACU observed test.

The first year's award went to Norton Motors when a standard ohv model was assembled from parts selected by an ACU engineer. It was then subjected to a twelve hour high speed test held at Brooklands wherein 18 World Records were set up.

The Maudes Trophy. The top picture shows the arduous conditions encountered. The bottom picture shows the Speed Twin at speed on Brooklands track.

FOR THE

MOST MERITORIOUS PERFORMANCE OF THE YEAR

UNDER A·C·U· OBSERVATION

1939

SNOW, ICE, MIST, & RAIN   WERE PRE-DOMINANT.

The "Maudes" Trophy was presented to the Auto Cycle Union in 1923, to be competed for annually by British motor cycle manufacturers and the award is made at the discretion of the A.C.U. Stewards for what is, in their estimation, the most meritorious performance of the year.

There is consistently keen competition amongst manufacturers for this award and tests are evolved in various strenuous forms, from time to time, each of which must

be held under observation by the A.C.U. These tests are for the purpose of demonstrating in a practical manner, the performance and reliability of motor cycles under all conceivable conditions.

No manufacturer can do more to prove his faith in the intrinsic merit of his products than to submit them to these stringent and exacting tests. Triumph motor cycles, it should be observed, have secured this highest-of-all award three times within the past six years.

"MAUDES" TROPHY

AWARDED TO

TRIUMPH

FOR THIRD TIME

WITHIN 6 YEARS

Ready for the off. The two machines before the high speed trial. A. Jefferies on the Speed Twin and I. Wicksteed on the Tiger 100. The pedal cycle in the background does not reflect on the machine's lap speeds

The Triumph test started in February 1939 when two brand new machines – one a Speed Twin and the other a Tiger 100 – were taken from dealers' stock completely at random by the ACU observer Mr. E.B. Ware. Mr Ware chose a Speed Twin from Messrs. Horridge & Wildgoose of Sheffield and a Tiger 100 from Messrs. Bryant of Biggleswade. These two motorcycles were subsequently marked and then taken back to the factory in Coventry.

The test got underway at 1 pm in the afternoon of Monday 27th February 1939. The riders were Reg Ballard and Bill Nicholls, on Speed Twin and Tiger 100 respectively.

Although new, the motorcycles were cruised at around 50/55 mph on the way from Coventry to John O'Groats being accompanied by a Triumph Dolomite car carrying the ACU observer and Mr. Headlam of Triumph, who was the event controller.

The first afternoon run was from Coventry to Carlisle, some 200 miles, and although torrential rain was encountered towards the end of the run, no problems were recorded.

Tuesday's run was from Carlisle to Inverness, some 275 miles, and this was accomplished at an average speed of 40 mph despite a diversion due to the road over Amulree being snowbound, forcing the route to go via Lockearnhead, Crianlarich, Glencoe, Fort William and to Inverness. The road through Glencoe proved rather tricky to negotiate due to packed snow. These conditions were endured for about 12 miles. Not long after this the T100 picked up a nail which punctured the rear tyre. The inner tube was repaired and unfortunately during refitting was punctured again, Excuses can be made as the riders must have been cold and weary by this time. The repairs were duly executed and when the motorcycle reached Inverness a new inner tube was fitted, mainly for safety reasons. The motorcycles had now covered nearly 500 miles so the oil tanks were drained, refilled and primary cases topped up.

Wednesday's route led to John O'Groats and back to Inverness with again route diversions due to snowbound roads on the outward run only as, by afternoon, the roads had become passable. The average speed for the day's run was 42 mph.

The run from Inverness south on Thursday was particularly unpleasant as the riders fought through heavy rain and sleet for hour after hour. Considering these conditions the average speed of 43 mph was very good.

At the night stop in Preston the rear chains were adjusted; primary chains were left untouched and they remained so throughout the 1800 miles.

The Friday run from Preston to Exeter with a strong wind and persistent drizzle again saw conditions far from ideal. From the lunchstop in Worcester the weather improved, much to everyone's relief.

Due to road repairs and negotiating Bristol the 38 mph average was the lowest of the whole trip despite some spirited riding.

Exeter to Exeter via Lands End was the route for Saturday and the only incident was when the Speed Twin slipped off its stand whilst parked. This resulted in a bent footrest which was replaced at the end of the day's run. Good average speeds were recorded on this run at nearly 47 mph.

The final day's run – Sunday – from Exeter to Brooklands was only 157 miles and this was achieved at an average of 50 mph, the motorcycles arriving at Brooklands around mid-day.

Apart from tightening a rocker feed oil pipe union nut and the previously mentioned puncture, this was the only time the spanners were laid on the motorcycles apart from normal routine servicing in the whole of the 1800 miles.

It was recorded that when inspected both motorcycles were in excellent order with no oil leaks other than slight smears. Total mileage was 1806 at an average speed of 42 mph. The two riders who had done such a good job in adverse conditions were relieved of the motorcycles as their riding work would be taken over by Freddie Clarke, Ivan Wicksteed, David Whitworth and Allan Jefferies, all speed men, for the six hour Brooklands test on Monday.

Before the endurance test on Brooklands track the machines were checked over in view of their 1806 miles. The tyres were changed to race type in the interest of safety. The valve clearances were checked but no adjustment was required. A new steering damper friction disc was fitted to the Tiger 100 due to over-enthusiastic greasing.

At 7.30 am the motorcycles were started and during warm-up the Tiger 100 speedometer needle behaved erratically so the speedometer was changed. Lodge R49 racing plugs were fitted and at 8 am the timekeeper, Mr. George Reynolds, started both motorcycles with Allan Jefferies on the Speed Twin and Ivan Wicksteed on the Tiger 100.

The two motorcycles ran steadily for several laps until the rear tyre of the Tiger 100 punctured on lap 10. A complete new rear wheel was fitted within four minutes but this lowered the average speed so a few laps at 82.83 mph were put in to re-establish a high average.

At the end of the first hour the Speed Twin had covered 74.2 miles and the Tiger 100 70.2 miles. After $1^{1}/_{2}$ hours a change of riders and refuelling took place, with Wicksteed being replaced by Whitworth and Jefferies by Clarke. All proceeded on schedule until the oil pipe to the pressure gauge on the Speed Twin leaked oil over the off-side of the bike. The pipe was hammered flat to prevent re-occurrence and Clarke returned to circle the track. In the second hour including pit stops the Tiger 100 was averaging 79 mph and the Speed Twin 74 mph. Just before the 3 hour stage Clarke came in with the hammered pipe seeping oil; this was resealed. Riders changed with Jefferies and Wicksteed out again. At 133 laps a plug was changed on the Speed Twin. Towards the end of the six hours the riders increased the lap speed with the Tiger 100 lapping at 88.45 mph and the Speed Twin at 84.41. At the

It's all over. The winning team but they were not to know it. This is March 1939 and the award was not declared until November. Left to right: E.B. Ware (ACU Observer) M.D. Whitworth (rider) I. Wicksteed (rider) A. Jefferies (rider) F. Clarke (rider) T. Wallis (Triumph fitter) E. Headlam (event controller)

end of the six hours average speeds including all stops were, Tiger 100 78.50 mph and Speed Twin 75.02 mph, with 471.5 and 450.25 miles covered respectively.

Next day the two motorcycles were ridden back to Coventry to record a total of 2383 miles for the Tiger 100 and 2362 miles for the Speed Twin.

Upon stripping the engines at the factory it was observed that the left-hand piston on the Speed Twin and the right-hand piston on the Tiger 100 had picked up slightly. Apart from this everything else was in perfect order.

As the original aim had been John O'Groats – Lands End up and down plus six hours at 70 + for the Speed Twin and 75 + for the Tiger 100 on standard dealer stock machines, one must conclude that Triumphs had triumphed.

The Maudes Trophy was awarded to the Triumph Engineering Co. Ltd. in November 1939.

1939 Successes

North West GP	1st
Enniskellen 100	1st + Fastest Lap
Belfast 100	1st + Record Lap
Cookstown 100	1st + Record Lap
Ascot Speedway USA Gold Cup	1st + Record Lap
Toronto Canada 50 Mile TT	1st

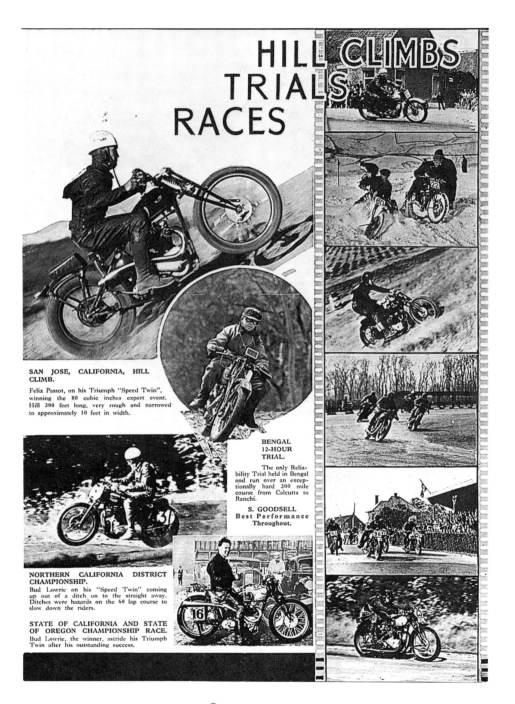

HILL CLIMBS
TRIALS
RACES

SAN JOSE, CALIFORNIA, HILL CLIMB.

Felix Passot, on his Triumph "Speed Twin", winning the 80 cubic inches expert event. Hill 300 feet long, very rough and narrowed to approximately 10 feet in width.

BENGAL 12-HOUR TRIAL.

The only Reliability Trial held in Bengal and run over an exceptionally hard 300 mile course from Calcutta to Ranchi.

S. GOODSELL Best Performance Throughout.

NORTHERN CALIFORNIA DISTRICT CHAMPIONSHIP.

Bud Lowrie on his "Speed Twin" coming up out of a ditch on to the straight away. Ditches were hazards on the 60 lap course to slow down the riders.

STATE OF CALIFORNIA AND STATE OF OREGON CHAMPIONSHIP RACE.

Bud Lowrie, the winner, astride his Triumph Twin after his outstanding success.

Overseas successes

36

The *Royal Tour*

THE TRIUMPH. MOTOR CYCLE ESCORT

THE BRITISH
KING AND QUEEN
IN
CANADA

A TRIUMPH motorcycle guard of honour, composed of twelve members of the "Princess Pats" regiment, was provided and carried out escort duty to Their Majesties in British Columbia on the occasion of their Tour of Canada and the U.S.A. in 1939.

The photographs reproduced show the guard of honour, the leaders of which are "Speed Twin" mounted, and two views taken *en route* in Victoria.

AND THE
U·S·A

Triumphs escort royalty

FEATURES

MOTOR. Triumph double high camshaft, vertical twin-cylinder air-cooled unit of advanced design, 2.48" bore by 3.15" stroke, 30.40 cubic inch displacement. Ports and moving parts polished. "H" section R.R.56 Hiduminium alloy connecting rods. Triumph patented big ends. Triumph patented built-up crankshaft incorporating integral balance weights with centrally disposed flywheel, mounted on heavy duty ball bearings. All auxiliaries gear-driven.

MOTOR SHAFT SHOCK ABSORBER The primary drive is by roller chain enclosed in oil bath case and the torque from the smooth twin-cylinder motor is still further evened out at low r.p.m. by an efficient harmonic action shock absorber, enabling the rider to tick along on top gear with a high compression motor with a smooth-as-silk transmission, without slipping the clutch.

TRANSMISSION. Triumph four-speed, silent on all gears, patented positive stop foot operated gear shift. This enables the rider instantly to change gear by a flick of the toe without removing his hand from the handle-bar. If, for example, the rider wishes to change down he simply de-clutches and presses the foot lever with his toe as far as it will go. The lever automatically returns to its normal position. Changing up is a reversal of this process. The Triumph gear shift has been proved to be the safest, simplest and most efficient yet devised.

CLUTCH. Triumph multi-disc type, running in oil bath, controlled by a hand lever on the bar. Light and sensitive it permits full use of the rider's legs at low speeds, either in traffic or on rough "going". It is possible for the rider to walk alongside and delicately control the drive to the back wheel by slightest hand pressure.

STEERING DAMPER. At very high speeds controllable friction on the steering column is an added safety measure. The Triumph steering damper is one of the many reasons why Triumph exceptional performance can be enjoyed to the full on any class of road, without fear of wobble or loss of control.

TANK. All-steel welded, enclosing rubber mounted instrument panel with oil gauge, ammeter, internal panel and inspection light. The tank holds sufficient gas for 300 miles and is designed to provide the rider with the most comfortable position, soft knee grips being recessed to prevent undue width.

SADDLE. Water-proofed surface mounted on a spring mattress and sprung by two generous coil springs, providing exceptional comfort and eliminating that familiar "seat ache" associated with long hours in the saddle.

BRAKES. Very efficient, enabling the motor cycle to be brought to a stop in 30 ft. at 30 m.p.h. At 90 m.p.h. they provide smooth retardation and halt the machine without skid or wobble.

FORK. Triumph girder spring fork of massive proportions, with a combination of compression and re-action springs, ensuring maximum comfort with safety at high speeds. Friction dampers ensure perfect front wheel road-holding on any surface at any speed.

ELECTRICAL AND IGNITION SYSTEM. Lucas 6-volt magneto combined with a generator giving 30 watts. Powerful headlight beam with a soft diffused light to pick out edges of track, making safe night riding. A lead-cell battery is mounted in an accessible position for topping up.

JIFFY STAND

TRIUMPH 4-SPEED TRANSMISSION

MULTI-DISC CLUTCH DISMANTLED

MOTOR SHAFT SHOCK ABSORBER DISMANTLED

BRAKE DRUM SECTIONED TO SHOW MECHANISM

STEERING DAMPER AND RESILIENTLY MOUNTED BAR

SPRING MATTRESS SADDLE

MAGNETO COMBINED WITH GENERATOR SECTIONED

THE TANK SHOWING INSTRUMENT PANEL & RECESSED KNEE GRIPS

THE ROBUST FORK SHOWING COMPRESSION & RE-ACTION SPRINGS

QUALITY IN EVERY COMPONENT PART

1940 Speed Twin features. British readers will have to pardon the American terms as this leaflet was written for the US market

38

1940 Model 5T Speed Twin
Engine Prefix 40-5T
Alterations for 1940

Engine
The oil feed to the crankshaft through the timing cover was redesigned to give better lubrication when the oil was hot. The redesign took the form of a bronze piston having a tubular extension situated in the end of the crankshaft. Under pressure better sealing was secured.

Larger clearances on the big-ends gave increased oil flow through the crankshaft, improving piston and cylinder wall oiling.

A 23 tooth engine sprocket was fitted to aid economy in view of the fuel shortages. Quoted mpg figures were 100 at 40 mph.

Frame
The frame head angle was changed to give more trail bringing the Speed Twin into line with the Tiger 100.

Forks
Redesigned forks had small check springs fitted each side of the main spring. These were so designed that at static position tension was at a minimum; tension increased as the fork deflected. A lighter main spring was used giving more sensitive action.

Petrol Tank
The capacity was increased to 4 gallons and commonised with that of the Tiger 100. Knee grips were changed to screw fixing type and the tank recessed to accommodate them without increasing the width. Colours remained as 1938 for the amaranth and gold, but an option for 1940 was black and chrome with ivory lining.

Switch Panel
There was a material change from Bakelite to steel due to the cracking of the panel. Finish of the steel pressing was in crystalline black, giving a crinkle finish.

Speedometer Cable
A new slimline cable was fitted – this being similar to the later post-war pattern.

Price
Fully equipped	£80 0s 0d

Extras
120 mph Speedometer	£2 15s 0d
120 mph Speedometer with 5 in dial	£5 5s 0d
Pillion footrests	7s 6d
Pillion seat	12s 6d
Prop stand	10s 0d
Valanced front and rear mudguards	12s 6d
Quickly detachable rear wheel	£2 0s 0d

A patent was taken out on 10.2.1939 in the name of the Triumph Engineering Co. Ltd. (Patent No. 524885) covering the Spring Hub and it was scheduled to be included in the 1940 programme. Some development work was carried out in 1939 and testing was well under way but prevailing circumstances prevented its inclusion into the 1940 motorcycle range. It was not until seven years later that it became available.

FUTURE DESIGN

These are extracts from a paper that Edward Turner read before the Institute of Automobile Engineers in 1943 when he was for a short time Technical Director of BSA Motor Cycles.

From it one can see that he was quite aware of all other design aspects and in some respects rather scathing over the racing design being fed through into the standard touring motorcycles.

Although he did not wish to see a two-wheeled car his ideal was certainly leaning towards the totally-enclosed two-wheeler, produced on a scale that everyone could afford.

"At a time when we are all preoccupied with the earnest job in hand of winning the war, it is impossible to escape from the significance of the oft repeated expression 'Winning the Peace'. This implies building a better world for all to enjoy and in the motorcycle world we will have an opportunity of making a useful contribution to this. It has been apparent however that the trend of development in the years leading up to the present war was in the wrong direction and tended to narrow the scope of appeal of the motorcycle.

The TT races provided a stimulus for design and, in fact, became a major objective for many manufacturers. It is therefore not surprising that the design requirements of this form of activity have had great influence on the standard products.

Logically, a vehicle, the design of which is inspired by specific activities, is bound to attract a market interested in these activities: thus we have an industry almost entirely supported by the sporting elements and consequently restricted in its appeal.

It is not suggested that the post-war motorcycle industry should not cater for the sport; on the contrary this section of development should and will receive considerable attention, but if motorcycle manufacture is ever to be one of Britain's staple industries, a type of motorcycle must be developed which will attract, by its utility, the ordinary pedestrian.

What can the power-driven two-wheeler offer that will induce the pedestrian to ride one, or a portion of car and cycle owners to prefer it as a means of transport or conveyance? In defining this we are defining the aims of post-war motorcycle design development.

1) The motorcycle is the most economical form of mechanically propelled vehicle. This applies to first cost, maintenance and running costs such as petrol, oil and rubber.
2) Handleability. This appears to be the only word to describe the facility with which the vehicle can be moved when not under power; it also covers the fact that traffic congestion is more easily negotiated with a motorcycle than with a car, and that the vehicle needs less parking space on the road or in the home.
3) It offers a most fascinating means of enjoying the open air.
4) In underdeveloped areas abroad, it is often the only means of conveyance due to its narrow width and ability to negotiate rough country.
5) It is the best means of training the rising generation in road sense and mechanical sense.
6) It is far and away the fastest vehicle available to man for a given capital expenditure.

Far too much emphasis has been laid on speed in the past, and manufacturers were forced to resort to very high compression ratios, freak timing diagrams, large clearances and other undesirable expedients to provide the necessary competitive performance. Under ordinary conditions 55 mph is, in the author's experience, about the maximum speed possible on a motorcycle without discomfort in good weather, and in designing a motorcycle for economical transport – as distinct from sport – there seems no point in making a machine capable of sustained speeds in excess of 55 mph.

It would appear that the motorcycle most likely to create a larger market must comply with the following:-

1) Be economical to buy and use.
2) Have good practical weather protection.
3) Be infinitely more silent both as regards exhaust and mechanical noise than has heretofore been accepted as standard.
4) Start easily and idle with certainty.
5) Be easy to clean and have as much of the 'works' enclosed as is possible.
6) Conform to the reliability standard that motor cars have taught the public to expect and the author would suggest as a minimum 10,000 miles without overhaul or adjustment. For such a relatively cheap vehicle 60,000 miles ought to be accepted as adequate life.
7) Handleability. The machine should be as light as it is possible to make it, consistent with reliability.
8) It should be less vulnerable and possess a maximum of stability".

He went on to discuss the merits of multi-cylinder engines and the induction problems associated with vee twins. He also remarked that four cylinder engines would be used in high priced machines in the sporting classes.

I think this brief resumé gives a good insight into the thoughts of the Speed Twin's designer and maybe shows why, in 1959, the Speed Twin went the way of near total enclosure.

SPEED TWIN: 1941-1944

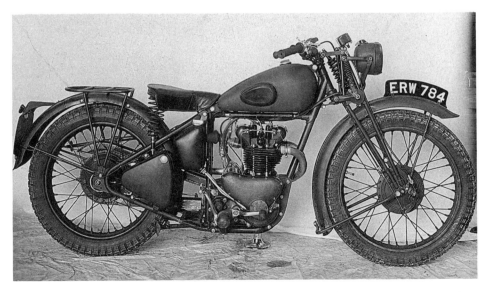

The 1941 350cc 3TWD – Note the alternator in the timing cover and the use of the petrol tank as part of the frame. Both these innovations would be featured on the Speed Twin at a later date 41

Due to Triumph being fully engaged in the war effort virtually no new models were introduced and it is fairly certain that no Speed Twins were produced in these years.

For the record it is well to recall that when the War Office asked manufacturers to produce a prototype to certain specifications laid down by them, Edward Turner was quick to respond. Triumph offered a 350cc ohv Twin with a weight of only 230 lb.

Approximately 25 of these machines were produced before the factory was blitzed out of existence. It was said that some of the 25 got as far as the Dunkirk beaches whilst the ones remaining at the factory were totally destroyed.

The only known remaining 3TWD 350cc twin is now lodged in the National Motor Museum at Beaulieu, being loaned by the Triumph Engineering Company some years ago. It keeps company with a 650cc Thunderbird that lapped Montlhéry at 100 mph.

A NEW ERA DAWNS
THE 1945 SPEED TWIN

When tooling up for the expected post-war boom the Triumph Engineering Company had the advantage of having an almost new factory at Meriden, the heart of England.

This new factory was surrounded by green fields and one could almost call it a factory in a garden. So rural were the surroundings that pigs were kept in sties adjacent to the steel stores and the canteen waste came in very useful for their upkeep. The Managing Director also had a cow which a certain member of the staff milked daily – quite a contrast milking cows, feeding pigs and building fast motorcycles, but in those days it was not thought strange or out of the ordinary.

The good fortune of a new factory has been brought about by the fact that the original Priory & Dale Street works had been bombed out of existence in the Coventry blitz of 1940.

The post-war programme announced by Triumph was not very radical, consisting of the two 500cc models, the 5T and T100, plus a newcomer, the 350cc 3T. For the first time in its history the Triumph Company had no single cylinder motorcycle in its range of models offered for sale. It is true that a 350cc ohv single, the 3HW, was sold in 1945 but these were essentially rebuilt or assembled from spare parts and were used to top up production when twin cylinder assembly was held up due to shortages.

A certain amount of re-styling and tidying up had taken place in the design, with the rear-mounted Magdyno giving way to separate components. The dynamo was now mounted at the front of the crankcase and the magneto flange-mounted at the rear. Both these units had their own independent drive by gear pinions.

A new hydraulically-damped telescopic front fork (I say new but actually Triumph had a tele fork running on test in 1942) replaced the previous girders, making the front of the machine look much sleeker and very much more tidy.

A 19 in front wheel was fitted to standardise the size. This replaced the previous 20 in wheel.

Rear suspension was to be offered as an optional extra in the form of the spring wheel. Cost of this would be £20.6s.5d. but this announcement was a little premature as it was not until September 1947 that this became a reality and production machines were so fitted.

A footchange pedal having a flattened, spoon-shaped foot lever with no rubber covering but having the Triumph logo in relief, was used. At the time the rubber shortage was acute and every little saved helped.

1945 model 5T Speed Twin
Engine Prefix 45-5T
Alterations for 1945

Engine
New crankcase giving provision for a front mounted dynamo and a rear flange fitting magneto (BTH) were substituted to the original design. Automatic ignition control via a BTH unit replaced the manually-operated type. The rocker oil drain external pipes were deleted and replaced by internal drillings in cylinder head and barrel. The rocker feed was reworked, the feed now being taken from a T junction in the return pipe at the oil tank. The engine breather was now a timed rotary valve driven by the inlet camshaft and vented to atmosphere by a flexible pipe on the left-hand side. The oil pressure release valve was redesigned, a piston type replacing the ball and spring arrangement used previously.

Front forks
Telescopic hydraulically damped front forks replaced the girders. Their total movement was $6^1/2$ inches.

Front wheel
A 19 in diameter rim replaced its earlier 20 in counterpart and a 3.25 in x 19 in Dunlop Universal tyre replaced the 3.00 in x 20 in tyre used previously.

Handlebar
A new handlebar bend was required to suit the telescopic forks.

Headlamp
The headlamp size was reduced to 7 inch diameter.

Oil tank
The capacity was increased to 8 pints and a 2 inch hinged filler cap fitted – falling into line with the one fitted to the Tiger 100.

A factory photograph of a 1945 Speed Twin showing an incorrectly painted front brake anchor plate and twin petrol taps

Electrical

The electrical system was 6 volt negative earth. Charging was by a Lucas E3H-RD dynamo via an automatic compensated voltage control box type MCR-L-4.

Carburettor

Choke operation was now by a spring loaded plunger operating on top of the mixing chamber. A throttle cable fitted with a 90° metal elbow provided better routing out of the twistgrip.

Price   £158 15s 0d

Extras

Speedometer   £4 8s 11d

1945 model 5T Speed Twin
Technical Data

Engine

As original specification.

Cylinder head

As original specification.

Valves

As original specification.

Valve guides

As original specification.

Valve springs

As original specification.

Cam followers

As original specification.

Valve clearance – cold

As original specification.

Valve timing

IVO	$26^{1}/_{2}°$	BTDC		
IVC	$69^{1}/_{2}°$	ABDC	0.020 in clearance for	
EWO	$61^{1}/_{2}°$	BBDC	checking timing	
EVC	$35^{1}/_{2}°$	ATDC		

Push rod

Material   Tubular steel with end caps top and bottom
Overall length   6.3000 in/6.325 in

Rockers

As original specification

Camshafts and Bearings

As original specifications

45

Camshafts and bearings

Bush diameter

LH bore	0.8125 in/0.8135 in
RH bore	0.874 in/0.875 in
LH outer	1.001 in/1.0015 in
RH outer	1.126 in/1.127 in
O/A length LH EX	0.932 in/0.942 in
LH IN	1.000 in/1.110 in
RH IN & EX	1.010 in/1.020 in

Cylinder barrel

Material	Cast iron
Cylinder bore diameter	2.4800 in/2.4805 in
Tappet guide bore	0.9985 in/0.9990 in
Max tolerable wear	0.007 in

Tappet block

Outer diameter	0.9995 in/1.000 in
Bore diameter	0.312 in/0.3125 in

Piston rings

As original specification.

Pistons

Clearance in cylinder bore at max dia (90° to gudgeon pin)	0.004 in/0.0045 in
Crown height from gudgeon pin centre 7.0:1	1 3/8 in
Gudgeon pin diameter	0.6882 in/0.6885 in

Connecting rods

Small end diameter	0.6905 in/0.6910 in
Big end diameter	1.4375 in/1.4385 in
Side clearance (fitted)	0.012 in/0.016 in
Length between centres	6.499 in/6.501 in
Bearing, big end	White metal

Crankshaft

As original specification.

Crankshaft bearing

As original specification.

Oil pump

As original specification.

Carburettor

Type	276 LH
Bore	15/16 in
Main jet	140
Needle jet	.107
Needle	No. 6
Needle position	3
Throttle valve	6/3
Float chamber	64/192

Ignition

Magneto	BTH – anti clock
Control	BTH automatic advance control
Timing	37° or $^3/_8$ in BTDC fully advanced
Points gap	0.012 in
Spark plug	Lodge H14 or Champion L11S
Plug gap	0.018 in
Thread size	14 mm
Reach	$^1/_2$ in

Transmission
Clutch:
As original specification.

Kickstart mechanism
As original specification.

Gearchange mechanism
As original mechanism.

Footchange spindle
As original specification.

Quadrant springs
As original specification.

Camplate plunger

Plunger dia	0.4360 in/0.4365 in
Housing bore diameter	0.4375 in/0.4380 in
Spring length	$2^1/_2$ in
No. of coils	22

Mainshaft
As original specification.

Layshaft
As original specification.

No. of teeth on pinions
As original specification.

Sprockets
As original specification.

Gear ratios – internal
As original specification.

Chains
As original specification.

Frame
As original specification.

Front fork

Stanchion diameter	1.3025 in/1.303 in
Top bush inner diameter	1.3065 in/1.3075 in
Top bush outer diameter	1.498 in/1.499 in

Top bush O/A length	0.995 in/1.005 in
Bottom bush inner diameter	1.2485 in/1.2495 in
Bottom bush outer diameter	1.4935 in/1.4945 in
Bottom bush O/A length	0.870 in/0.875 in
Fork leg bore	1.498 in/1.500 in
Spring free length	20 in ± $^1/_8$ in
Wire diameter	0.160 in

Wheels
Rim size
    Front and rear   WM2 x 19 in
Tyres
    Front   3.25 in x 19 in Dunlop Universal
    Rear   3.50 in x 19 in Dunlop Universal
    Pressures – front   18 psi
              rear   16 psi

Wheel bearings
Front ball journal   20 x 47 x 14 mm
Rear taper roller $^9/_{16}$ in x 1$^3/_4$ in x $^{13}/_{16}$ in x $^9/_{16}$ in outer

Spokes
Front
LH inner 10 off	8$^{11}/_{32}$ in x 10G 88°
LH outer 10 off	8$^{11}/_{32}$ in x 10G 90°
RH inner 10 off	6$^3/_8$ in x 10G 83°
RH outer 10 off	6$^3/_8$ in x 10G 96°

Rear
LH inner 10 off	8$^3/_4$ in x 9G 76°
LH outer 10 off	8$^3/_4$ in x 9G 100°
RH inner 10 off	8$^3/_4$ in x 9G 76°
LH outer 10 off	8$^3/_4$ in x 9G 100°

Wheel offset
Front – dimension from drum edge to
centre of rim   2$^3/_{16}$ in
Rear – dimension from outer edge of
sprocket to centre of rim 3$^5/_{32}$ in

Speedometer
Type   Smiths S464/3/L with rev dial calibrated in mph.
Cable length   49 in

Electrical
Dynamo	Lucas E3H RD 40 Watt
Voltage	6 volt
Earth	Negative
Battery	Lucas PUW7E/4 12 amh/hr
Horn	Lucas Altette HF 1234
Headlamp	Lucas 7 in D42 CPR
Tail lamp	Lucas MT110
Bulb main	6v 24/30 or 24/24
Bulb pilot	6v 3W
Bulb speedo	6v 3W
Bulb tail	6v 3W
Bulb inspection	6v 3W

Dimensions

Wheelbase	54 in
O/all length	84 in
O/all width	28^1/$_2$ in
Seat height	29^1/$_2$ in
Weight	361 lb.
Ground clearance	6 in

Lubrication

Engine – summer	SAE 40-50
Winter	SAE 20-30
Gearbox	EP90
Primary case	SAE 20
Telescopic fork	SAE 20 or 30
Grease	Castrol LM

Capacities

Fuel tank	4 Imp gall (18 litre)
Oil tank	6 Imp pint (3.5 litre)
Gearbox	2/3 Imp pint (400 cc)
Primary case	^{1}/$_2$ Imp pint (300 cc)
Telescopic fork	1/6 Imp pint (100 cc)

Left hand threads
Camshaft pinion nuts

Price	£139 14s 0d
Extras Smiths 120 mph speedometer	£4 8s 10d

Thoughts and comments about the 1947 models

The following is a memo from the Managing Director Edward Turner to his works team giving his thoughts and comments on the coming 1947 season. Followers who are conversant with the design history of the Speed Twin will note that a few of the items actually did get incorporated in the production machine whilst others, sad to say, never saw the light of day. In all probability the items could not be manufactured cheaply enough and therefore would have raised the price of the machine, something that could not be tolerated.

"The time has come when we must consider 1947 improvements. The demand for our products today fortunately does not make radical changes essential, but it would be desirable to introduce certain modifications to increase the appeal of the machine and show an indication that we are not resting on our laurels. Any contemplated changes must not interfere with the main manufacturing equipment, neither should they increase the cost of the machine. On the other hand, any improvement that could reduce the cost of the machine without impairing its efficiency or lowering its standard would be an advantage.

I would welcome any suggestions in addition to those outlined below, which are only for consideration.

Gearbox:	Modification to cam plate to provide easily found neutral, either below bottom gear or other alternative.
Clutch:	Sooner or later it will ne necessary to abandon the cork clutch and experiments should be conducted once more with fabric inserts with very much increased spring pressure and a proportional

	reduction in axial push-rod movement by increasing the leverage of the operating mechanism.
Handlebar:	This should be cleaner and have two built-in switches and internal wiring. The dip switch and horn button should be on the left and the cut-out button on the right.
Horn:	We must draw a small streamlined horn to mount on the front fork and try all electrical manufacturers with a view to buying this horn at a keen price.
Instrument panel:	It would be a great advantage if we could remove the instrument panel from the tank completely and locate it on the crown of the fork.
Saddle:	A new pan seat on a metal base with sorbo insulation should be drawn out for Dunlop's Experimental Department to pick up as a development. This they are willing to do.
Guards:	The problem here is to produce new guards giving more effective mud protection without increasing the price and withal retaining an elegant appearance.
	I would like to see a layout for the whole of the rear guard to be detached in one piece for wheel removal, jointing at the back stays, so as to remove the ugly gap in the guard at the back, simplify the stays, and have an entirely flush rear guard surface. Front guard – some valance which would either be in one piece with the guard, thereby not increasing the price, or alternative suggestions.
Stand:	It will be absolutely vital for us to produce a quick-operating prop stand for 1947. Please obtain the stand used by AMC as a basis for discussion.
Twist grip:	Quick-opening twist grip on the helical principle to enable an internal cable to go through the bar would be a neater job. The present twist grip, though successful, is not entirely suitable for small choke carburettors and the cable is untidy.
Petrol indicator:	A simple device to enable the rider to see at a glance how much petrol there is in the tank would be an advantage.
Chain cover:	Although I do not anticipate going in for an enclosed rear chain for 1947, any improvement in the present chainguard arrangements, particularly in its effect on water, should be tried out.
Carburettor:	I would like to see experiments brought well forward for fitting a Zenith or Solex carburettor on our machines for 1947. I believe these could be bought at an even lower price than Amal and they would have the advantage of enabling us to use a piano wire push/pull twist grip.

On receipt of your further suggestions, which will have careful consideration, I will draw up a schedule for design modifications for 1947 which should be made, tested and released for production not later than the end of July for inclusion in our range early in October, although these will be publicised in the press early in September".

Signed – E. Turner
Managing Director

(Facing page)

Alex Oxley did a series of cartoons for Triumph. They were quite amusing in their day and it illustrates how gentle advertising was at that time

1946 model 5T Speed Twin
Engine Prefix 46-5T
Alterations from 1945

Engine
Compression ratio lowered to 6.5:1.
Engine sprocket reverted back to 22 teeth.

Carburettor
Float chamber 1 AT.

Gearbox
From engine number 74760 a change in the dogs of the mainshaft 2nd gear to the mainshaft 4th gear was introduced to provide easier gear engagement.

Providing the gears are kept as matching pairs (new or old) they are fully interchangeable.

Frame
No change.

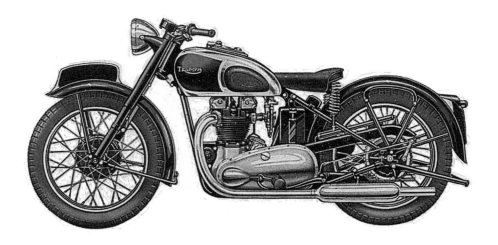

Left hand view of the 1946 Speed Twin

Oil tank
Early models had an 8 pint oil tank with a 2 inch hinged filler cap – later models reverted to pre-war type i.e. 6 pint with screwed alloy cap.

Apart from these small changes it was a period of marking time on modifications with the emphasis on trying to catch up with outstanding orders.

Price   £158 15s 0d

Extras
Smiths 120 mph speedometer   £4 8s 11d

Very little change to the specification took place for the 1947 season.

It was a very difficult time for manufacturers as Britain had not fully recovered from the ravages of war and no real manufacturing rhythm could be achieved due to shortage of raw materials. In actual fact steel was rationed and this resulted in stop-start production. It was in this difficult environment that the Triumph Managing Director, Edward Turner, issued this statement to support his no change policy.

"We believe that the best contribution Triumphs can make to the national recovery is to supply Triumph Twins to would-be owners, and they number many thousands, with the least possible delay. We shall continue our successful range of models unchanged for 1947 in order to avoid the production hold-ups which would be unavoidable were any other policy to be followed, especially under present day conditions."

That he was quite correct to take this route was borne out when it was recorded that despite the most strenuous efforts, supply never caught up with demand.

1946 Speed Twin
Road Test Impressions

The first post-war test of the Speed Twin praised the change to telescopic front forks both from the rider comfort viewpoint and the much tidier general appearance. Also praised was the four gallon tank which had replaced the three gallon of pre-war days, although to be correct this had been specified for 1940.

The Speed Twin engine was always tidy in appearance but this was improved by the removal of the external oil drain pipes which used to lead from the rocker boxes. This oil return was now internal, drillings in the head and barrel carrying the oil away.

The handlebar control layout was complimented for the minimum of levers. For example, the ignition lever had been dispensed with as had the air control or choke lever. A spring-loaded plunger sited on top of the carburettor mixing chamber controlled the air slide whilst the ignition advance and retard was looked after by an automatic centrifugal device attached to the magneto drive.

In the interests of providing reliability the compression ratio was reduced from 7.0:1 to 6.5:1 to suit the "Pool" petrol available (approx. 72 octane). This did not seem to affect the overall performance very much and Mr. Turner, Triumph's Managing Director, was quoted as saying he believed the Speed Twin had all the speed and more that the average rider needs. He was quite prepared to cast away a knot or two if in so doing he could achieve, on an inferior grade of fuel, a performance even smoother and a machine even nearer his ideal of efficient simplicity than he had in the earlier models.

That the particular tester was taken by the Speed Twin may be somewhat of an understatement as he used words like exhilarating, sympathy with the machine, hair-line steering and super adequate braking to sum up the impressions after a few miles.

One slight criticism concerned rear wheel hop and it was thought that footrests further towards the rear may have alleviated this tendency.

Braking figures were good at 35 feet for the front brake alone with 29 feet for both brakes from 30 mph. Due to the leverage available and maybe a light rear end the rear brake could lock the rear wheel under relatively light application of the pedal.

In the maximum speed and the flying quarter mile the new Speed Twin lost a shade to its predecessor but made up for this by providing remarkable flexibility and silky performance with 17 mph in top gear being used without snatch, even when accelerating from this speed on full throttle.

This smooth power made effortless high average speed miles possible at an economical 66 – 77 mpg.

At the conclusion of the test no oil leaks were visible, the general finish was above reproach and all the instruments were in full working order. Obviously the tester did not like the carburettor-mounted choke lever as he could not reach it with a gloved hand and it was, by its nature, either full on or off with no progressive setting. He redeemed himself by adding that the Speed Twin is to be seen as one of the most handsome motorcycles ever produced. With its clean lines and compactness it looks, and is, functionally correct.

Maximum Speeds

Top Gear (5 to 1)	90 mph =	5850 rpm	37 4/5 secs.
Third Gear (6 to 1)	84 mph =	6670 rpm	27 4/5 secs.
Second Gear (8.65 to 1)	62 mph =	6919 rpm	12 3/5 secs.

Measured Quarter Mile

Flying start	86.6 mph
Standing start	50.7 mph

Fuel Consumption

Urban	66 mpg
Overall	77 mpg

Braking from 30 mph

Front brake only	35 feet
Rear brake only	54 feet
Both brakes	29 feet

The victory parade with the King and Queen on the saluting base as the Speed Twins pass by. London, June 8th 1946.

1947 model 5T Speed Twin
Engine Prefix 47-5T
Alterations from 1946

Engine
No change.

Carburettor
The float chamber was changed over to the left hand side of the mixing chamber. This entailed a new carburettor with a throttle stop screw and pilot mixture screw on the right hand side. New carburettor No. 276 BN/1AT.
Mixing chamber now No. 76/132M.

Frame
No change but a prop stand was offered as a bolt on extra – to be fitted under the chaincase as the pre-war prop stand could not be fitted due to the dynamo taking the required space.

Headlamp
The headlamp shell was now painted amaranth red and the rim was chrome plated.

Price   £180 6s 10d

Extras
    Smiths 120 mph speedometer   £5 1s 8d

The 1947 sales brochure illustration showed for the first time the spring wheel. Note also the 'bare' footchange gear pedal

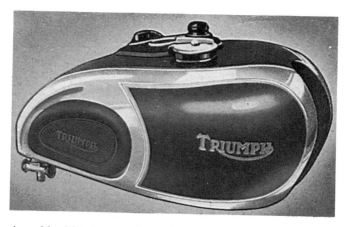

Tank panel and lining detail

A wealth of detail here with identical horn and ignition cut-out push button switches, dip switch and large ebonite steering damper knob

TRIUMPH

The Best Motorcycle in the World

TRIUMPH ENGINEERING CO., LTD.,
Meriden Works, Allesley, COVENTRY

Two views of what Johnson Motors USA thought the Speed Twin should look like. Note the twin carburettor set-up

1948 model 5T Speed Twin
Engine Prefix 48-5T
Frame Nos:- TF 15001 to TF 24765
Engine Nos:- 88227–4.9.1947 to 102160–19.10.1948
Alterations from 1947

For 1948 no engine changes took place but during the season year several changes took place to the motorcycle parts.

Due to circumstances outside the company's control these changes could not be introduced at the onset of the season but were brought in as and when convenient.

Gearbox
With the introduction of the spring wheel an alternative to the original rear wheel-driven speedometer gearbox had to be found. The solution was to provide a speedometer gearbox attached to the rear of the gearbox and driven from the rear of the final drive gearbox sprocket. When this was specified the cable length was reduced to 49 inches.

Footchange lever
The footchange lever regained a rubber, covering the foot part. This, of course, had the Triumph logo moulded in the rubber.

Speedometer cable
A reduced 49 inch length speedometer cable was fitted from TF 15069 on September 16th.

Steering damper
The front fork steering damper was reduced in diameter and the material changed from ebonite to aluminium alloy embossed with the Triumph logo. Fitted from TF 15530 on October 1st.

Spring wheel
The first Speed Twin to be equipped with the optional spring wheel was TF 15069 on September 16th.

Front mudguard
A new front mudguard was fitted with two detachable front stays and had a raised pressed front edge to aid waterproofing. It was fitted from TF 16227 on November 4th

Rear mudguard
The new rear mudguard was wider and had only two fixing stays each side. It was detachable from under the seat and was fitted from TF 17790 on January 1st.

Rear frame
A new rear frame to accept the above rear mudguard was fitted from TF 17790 on January 1st.

Voltage control (Lucas MCR-1)
The new fixing comprised a nut and bolt fitting across the rear sub-frame, to two small welded brackets from TF 17790 on January 1st.

Rear number plate
The rear number plate top portion was reshaped to provide a hand-hold whilst using the rear stand. This was made necessary by the deletion of the two side handles fitted to the earlier rear mudguard.

Front number plate
The front number plate incorporated a minor change whereby the styling beading was cast on to the actual plate; prior to this beading had been detachable.

A 1948 Speed Twin showing the new front and rear mudguards

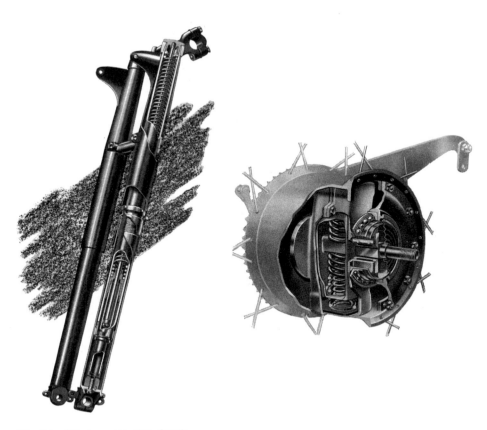

The Speed Twin suspension details

Carburettor
The throttle valve was changed to a 6/3½ from TF 23324 on August 17th.

Headlamp
The headlamp was fitted with a domed glass.

Ignition
Plug caps were introduced as a standard fitment.

Weight
With optional spring wheel fitted 374 lb.

Price	£180 6s 10d

Extras

Smiths 120 mph speedometer	£5 1s 8d
Prop stand	£1 11s 8d
Spring wheel	£20 6s 5d

THE SPEED TWIN IN THE 1948 INTERNATIONAL SIX DAYS TRIAL

After the cessation of hostilities (1939-1945) the International Six Days Trial was re-introduced, 1948 being the first post-war event. The trial had been a great pre-war feature and the rivalry between England, Germany and Italy in particular had been quite intense.

The 1948 event was to take place in San Remo, Italy, and Triumph decided to build and enter a team of three, mounted on Speed Twins. These were in essence standard machines but as an aid to lightness and reliability due to the expected hot climate, alloy cylinder barrels and heads had been fitted, borrowed from the Triumph war-time generator set.

Riders for these machines had been decided and were, in no particular order of merit, P.H. Alves, A. Jefferies, and A.F. Gaymer, all of whom were at that time Triumph works riders in trials and scrambles, plus in Jefferies' case a road racer too. Jefferies had won the British Experts Trial of 1938, Triumph-mounted of course, but not on a Speed Twin.

All reports indicated that the San Remo event was to be the most difficult yet staged, with need to contend with swirling dust and rocky cobbled tracks. Many competitors were forced out by these arduous conditions but the Trumph team were obviously up to it and finished the event without losing a single mark.

For this achievement each rider received a gold medal and they were also presented with a manufacturer's team prize. The manufacturer's team prize was one of only two awarded, foreign riders taking the other.

This was a most creditable performance by the three riders and their Speed Twins, showing again the motorcycle's reliability and justifying the Company's faith in its twin cylinder design.

A sequel to this achievement came when the buying public wanted to purchase a ready-made competition Triumph. The company appraised the situation and from various models built a suitable machine was evolved which, of course, after the 1948 success just had to be called the Trophy. Possibly many readers will know or have fond recollections of it.

Registration numbers of the three International Six Day Trial Speed Twins were:-

HHP 90   –   HHP 91   –   HHP 92

The motorcycles were built on July 22nd 1948 with the following frame, engine and gearbox numbers-

TF 22661	5T 99308	99634
TF 22662	5T 99240	99636
TF 22663	5T 99367	99635

1949 model 5T Speed Twin
Engine Prefix 5T-9
Frame Nos:- TF 25115 to TF 33615
Engine Nos:- 102581–2.11.1948 to 113386–6.10.1949
Alterations from 1948

A major change in the appearance of the Speed Twin took place for 1949 with the introduction of the nacelle. This nacelle housed the light switch and ammeter, therefore the tank panel was no longer required.

Engine
The oil pressure release valve was modified and fitted with an indicator button. This was made necessary by the deletion of the oil pressure gauge.

The engine breather discharge pipe was relocated to point downwards from an interference fit metal pipe in the crankcase. A flexible rubber pipe was added to this pipe to take the crankcase fumes into the atmosphere. The compression was reinstated to 7.0:1 with the slightly better quality fuel that had become available.

Gearbox
All models were now fitted with the speedometer drive taken from the gearbox sprocket. Previously this had only applied to spring wheel equipped models.

Carburettor
Choke control was changed from the spring loaded plunger to cable operation, with the control lever situated on the left hand chainstay just under the seat. Carburettor no: 276/DK/1AT.

Front forks
The upper end of the fork was all virtually new for 1949. The nacelle top unit housed the light switch on the right with the ammeter on the left. Situated between these two items was the ignition cut-out button. To the fore of these was the speedometer. An adaptor ring was fitted to take the standard headlamp rim and glass.

Due to a shortage of steel pressings the first 800 (5T and T100) lower nacelle units were alloy castings.

Handlebars
A new shaped handlebar bend was used to suit the nacelle.

Controls
The spring and plunger friction device on the twistgrip was dropped and a knurled adjustable knob with friction spring introduced.

The dip switch was now fitted to the front brake clamp bracket and had a chrome plated surround.

The horn push button was relocated and was screwed direct into a threaded hole in the handlebar on the left hand side.

61

Speed Twins for the Swedish army. The new for 1949 nacelle and petrol tank with luggage rack are well illustrated

Although a T100, this bird's eye view was too good to leave out, giving as it does front fork details and oil tank transfer positioning

Petrol tank
The petrol tank switch panel was deleted and was replaced by a chrome-plated three bar parcel grid which was offered as an optional extra. When the parcel grid was not fitted, the threaded pommel holes were plugged by small rubber grommets.

Air filter
An air filter was specified as standard, being fitted between the battery carrier and seat down tube. The battery carrier back strap was stepped to accommodate the filter.

Toolbox
This remained essentially the same but the threaded lid retaining knob gave way to a push and twist DZUS fastener.

Footbrake pedal
The rubber pad covering the foot part of the lever was deleted, leaving the bare metal with a ridged line appearance.

Electrical
The dynamo output was increased by the use of a 60 watt E3L-L1-0 unit, recognisable by its longer length than the previous 40 watt type. Introduction frame number was TF 29130 on April 4th.

With the new longer dynamo a new Lucas regulator box was required, type MCR-2-L.

The rear light cable was armoured and routed on to the inside of the mudguard, down the centre rib, to emerge through grommets, aimed at tidying up the rear end.

Speedometer

Basically as previous but with a new bezel to accommodate nacelle fitting and having a rear or bottom-mounted trip control extended to protrude below the nacelle.

Price   £180   6s 10d

Extras

Smiths 120 mph speedometer	£5 1s 8d
Prop stand	£1 11s 8d
Spring wheel	£20 6s 5d

1949 Speed Twin
Road Test Impressions

The basic details of the 1949 Speed twin were as 1946 with additional items such as the front fork nacelle and the spring wheel giving the bike a new look.

Rider comfort was enhanced by the Spring Wheel and the tester found that it absorbed all but the most severe bumps taking all the punishment itself and transmitting nothing to the rider.

Criticism of the choke location on the 1946 test had been heeded and the control was now located on the left, under the seat. It was a location that whilst much better than before still earned a remark from the tester that it took a little getting used to.

Starting was exceptional with never more than two digs on the kickstart required, even on a cold morning. When cold, a small amount of throttle was required but with the engine warm it would always start on the pilot jet with the throttle shut.

Main road cruising was effortless. At 55 mph it was difficult to hear the exhaust note and induction hiss was completely eliminated with the new air filter arrangement. A slight movement of the body was all that was necessary to negotiate main road bends. When these were sharper than anticipated the Speed Twin could be heeled over with complete confidence.

The Speed Twin is essentially a top gear motorcycle, the other three ratios only being required when traffic congestion and towns were encountered. Acceleration was of a high order, third gear taking one past baulking traffic at 70 mph.

So smooth was the engine and transmission that no snatch could be felt at 20 mph in top gear and it was possible with a little discretion to accelerate to maximum from this speed without a gear change.

Braking was adequate but it was felt a little more bite would be advantageous. Generally however the brakes could be commended on the progressive way they did their job.

Gear changes were of the usual Triumph excellence and providing a slight pause was made when changing up in the lower ratios, noiseless changes resulted. This did not apply to the change between third and top which could be made as fast as the pedal could be moved, both up and down. Clutch operation was excellent, being light in action without a trace of slip or drag.

The compression ratio had been reinstated at 7.0:1 without any increase in top speed over the 1946 model. This was due to the fitting of an air filter although the standing start figure had improved.

At the conclusion of the test no oil leaks were apparent and apart from travel stains collected during a very wet period the engine and gearbox were as clean as at the beginning.

64

Criticisms were few and were confined to the choke lever position, the prop stand being inaccessible to the foot when in the retracted position and the fact that the speedometer was not too easy to read when the needle was between fifty and eighty miles per hour.

Maximum Speeds

Top Gear (5 to 1)	88 mph	5618 rpm	39 secs.
Third Gear (6 to 1)	84 mph	6670 rpm	26 secs.
Second Gear (8.65 to 1)	63 mph	6930 rpm	12 1/5 secs.

Measured Quarter Mile

Flying start	84.9 mph
Standing start	54.5 mph

Fuel Consumption

Urban	67 mpg
Overall	74 mpg

Braking from 30 mph

Front brake only	37 feet
Rear brake only	49 feet
Both brakes	30 feet

1950 model 5T Speed Twin
Engine Prefix 5T
Engine and frame numbers 1009N–17.10.1949 to 16084N–2.11.1950
Alterations from 1949

Reference to the year of manufacture within the engine number was deleted as it was causing embarrassment to overseas dealers who on occasions were still selling the previous season's models.

Taking advantage of this change an opportunity to tidy up the numbering system was implemented. This resulted in engine and frame numbers being identical from this date onwards.

Engine

The external overhead rocker oil drain pipes were reintroduced as the introduction of the 650 cc 6T model made this necessary. With its larger cylinder bore, no room was left for the internal oil drain drillings.

The oil pump was modified to give increased oil flow.

A different contour to the shock absorber cam was designed to give a progressive spring load.

Gearbox

A completely re-designed gearbox was introduced as it was considered the original type would not be adequate for the 650 6T.

This new gearbox had a live layshaft of much increased strength (this had been the previous box's weakness). It also had provision for the speedometer drive to be taken from the right hand end of the shaft through a right angle drive to emerge from the front of the inner cover. The re-design also incorporated a full garter oil seal on the final drive sprocket, to aid oil sealing.

It should be noted that none of the shafts and gears are interchangeable between the two gearboxes.

The new gearboxes gave different internal ratios due to the gear teeth differences:

4th	1.00	2nd	1.69
3rd	1.19	1st	2.44

Many Automobile Association box sidecars were hauled along by Speed Twins such as the one shown here. This one is brand new and is awaiting collection from the works car park

Gearbox gears
   Number of teeth

Layshaft		Mainshaft
20	4th	26
22	3rd	24
26	2nd	20
30	1st	16

Petrol tank

Due to overseas problems of internal rusting, the petrol tanks lost their chrome plate. Tanks were now all one colour. In the case of the Speed Twin this was amaranth red.

New horizontal fluted styling bands were fitted from the forward edge of the knee grip to the edge of the tank. The raised flutes were in chrome with the background painted red. Retained by the same fixing screws were two small chrome plated Triumph badges with the Triumph name and a raised painted background.

A more normal plain push and twist cam action Ceandes filler cap replaced the hinged lever type.

The parcel grid which previously had been an optional extra became standard equipment.

Rear suspension

Due to some failures of the cup and cone bearings in the spring wheel a new design was introduced and designated the Mk II. Its main feature was the large (3^1/$_2$ in diameter) journal ball races. Externally it was easily identified by the use of ribbed end plates.

Seat

To give an improved ride, barrel shaped springs were fitted to the saddle. These gave a variable rate. The Triumph patented Twinseat was offered as an optional extra, replacing the single saddle and pillion pad.

Electrical		Extras	
Dynamo Type	E3L-L1-0	Prop stand	£1 11s 9d
		Pillion seat	£1 11s 9d
Speedometer cable		Twinseat	£2 4s 6d
Length	44 inch	Pillion footrests	£1 0s 4d
		Spring wheel	£20 6s 5d
Price	£185 8s 5d		

The new tank badges for 1950 and the optional extra Twinseat are featured here

1951 model 5T speed Twin
Engine Prefix 5T
Engine and Frame Numbers 840NA–21.11.1950 to 15192NA–16.11.1951
Alterations from 1950

Engine

A new fully machined crankshaft with heavier bobweights was used for greater consistency.

The camwheel pinions now incorporated three keyways to commonise with the T100 model.

The crankshaft right hand bearing was changed from a ball journal to a roller bearing which was capable of carrying higher loadings.

Cam followers with Stellite faced tips were fitted to combat premature wear.

Taper faced piston rings were used to give quicker bedding in. The connecting rods now featured a strengthened section, also to commonise with the T100.

The balance factor was changed to 64%.

68   A radio-equipped Speed Twin. The stop light switch was an optional extra

A nice advertisement placed in *The Motor Cycle* **emphasing the clean lines of the Triumph**

Carburettor
A new float chamber number 1ATM was now fitted. The complete carburettor number was 276 DK/1AT/M.

Front brake
To improve the effectiveness of the front brake a Mehenite cast iron brake drum was fitted, replacing the pressed steel composite pattern previously used.

Speedometer
The speedometer dial was recalibrated to bring the 30-70 mph section to the top of the instrument, to provide easier reading. Coded S467/99/L, it replacing the earlier S467/19 type.

Electrical
A new tail lamp was fitted, with a tapering body that gave a larger reflective area – Lucas number 53216A. This lamp could have a stop lamp incorporated with the switch controlled by the rear brake rod via a spring.

Price	£185 8s 5d

Extras

Spring wheel	£20 6s 5d	Twinseat	£2 4s 6d
Prop stand	£1 11s 9d	Valanced mudguards	both available to
Pillion footrests	£1 0s 4d	Heel and toe footchange lever	special order
Pillion seat	£1 11s 9d		

A late 1951 advertisement showing painted handlebars which also featured in 1952

1952 Model 5T 1954 Speed Twin
Engine Prefix 5T
Engine and Frame Numbers
16000NA – 18.11.1951 to 22000 – 2.1.1952 then 26096 – 24.3.1952 to 31901 –
19.8.1952
Alterations from 1951

The most obvious change for 1952 was the restyled front fork nacelle. This was now larger in diameter, giving the motorcycle a much bolder look, and it also had a small pilot light slung under the main headlamp where there had been louvres or vents.

A minor change involved the shortening of the fork springs to drop the front end slightly when the motorcycle was stationary. Always on the alert for what he called 'eyeability' Edward Turner disapproved of the painted section of the fork being broken by the seal holder showing. The slightly shorter spring overcame this and everyone was happy.

Apart from engine numbering altering slightly by losing the NA suffix no changes were made to this unit.

The barrel-shaped seat springs and tapering rear lamp introduced in 1951 are carried through but new for 1952 is the larger diameter nacelle

Gearbox and transmission stayed as 1951 with no changes recorded.

A new frame was introduced having an "eye" in the seat down-tube to provide a straight entry from the air filter to the carburettor. Along with this modification came a new 'D' shaped Vokes air filter mounted between the battery and oil tank. The exit tube and carburettor connecting rubber went directly through the frame tube eye.

How the new air filter goes through the 'eye' in the frame tube

A slight modification to the oil tank resulted in the pommel in the back of the tank being deleted and replaced by a welded-on strap fixed to the rear mudguard. This was aimed at reducing tank failures due to splitting at the pommel fixing.

The brake pedal footpad was reduced in size being almost square in shape and having a pinnacled finish.

The rear wheel brake drum and sprocket were now integral and of cast iron, replacing the bolted-on type sprocket and separate brake drum.

Visually, the petrol tank differed in as much as a central weld now ran from front to rear. This was due to an entirely new method of manufacture where two deep drawn pressings were made and joined in the centre. This had the benefit of having no bottom seams on the outside base of the tank, so avoiding leakage problems.

The bridge pipe connecting the left and right hand sides of the tank was dispensed with, being very bothersome when tank removal was required as the fuel had to be drained off first. Its place was taken by a blanking plug in the right hand threaded boss and a normal main and reserve tap on the left. Also the braided steel fuel pipe was replaced by one of water clear plastic.

With the new air filter being placed more centrally, the battery carrier was replaced by the pre-1947 type which had a straight back bracket instead of one of the cranked 'dog leg' pattern.

Positive earth was introduced on Triumphs because the motor trade was of the opinion that less terminal corrosion took place when this arrangement was used. A sealed beam 7 inch diameter light unit was fitted in the new nacelle unit giving far better lighting than previously with the added advantage that many car light units would fit the motorcycle. A new pilot lamp completed the change.

Finish of the 1952 Speed Twin was adversely affected by the severe restrictions laid down by the authorities on the use of nickel due to a world shortage of this metal. Parts that had by long tradition always been chrome plated (over a base nickel plating) had to be painted and on the Speed Twin this meant – handlebars painted amaranth red, wheel rims painted silver with red centres lined in gold, kickstart lever, clutch operating arm and exhaust pipe finned clips cadmium plated.

It is not possible to state with certainty the engine and frame numbers of the models affected but it is certain that it was taking effect in August 1951 just prior to the start of the 1952 season and it could well have run into the start of the 1953 season. Most restored 1952 models one sees around today take no account of this utilitarian finish.

Engine

The engine number system was changed. After 20306NA the suffix letters were deleted and numbers only used on the frame and engine. The numbers remained identical on both engine and frame.

Frame

The "eye" type of frame was introduced from 16000NA.

Air filter

The new 'D' type of Vokes air filter was introduced from 16000NA.

Oil tank

A new oil tank with revised fixing was introduced from 16000NA. The vent pipe from the oil tank was now taken into the rear of the primary chaincase via two small flexible rubber connections joined by a steel pipe. Prior to this the vent had been down the seat tube with any overflow becoming a trifle messy where it exited.

Front forks

A new nacelle unit and shorter fork springs ($^3/4$ inch less) were introduced from 16000NA.

Brake pedal

Now fitted with a smaller footpad, introduced from 16000NA.

Rear wheel

An integral brake drum and rear wheel sprocket was introduced from 16000NA.

Petrol tank

A new tank was fitted having a visible central weld and a blanking plug from 16000NA.

Petrol pipes

Water clear plastic pipes were fitted from 16000NA.

Battery carrier

A straight backed carrier was fitted from 16000NA.

Electrical

A new 7 inch sealed beam headlight and underslung pilot lamp were introduced from 16000NA. Positive earth was introduced from 19706NA.

Price	£206 11s 2d
Extras	
Spring wheel	£20 8s 11d
Twinseat	£2 4s 9d
Pillion seat	£1 12s 0d
Pillion footrests	£1 0s 6d
Prop stand	£1 12s 0d

Model 5T 1953 Speed Twin
Engine Prefix 5T
Engine and Frame Numbers 33868 – 14.10.1952 to 45575 – 6.10.1953
Alterations from 1952

A major change for 1953 was the adoption of coil ignition with a charging system by AC alternator mounted on the left hand crankshaft and chaincase.

These early alternator models had two switches mounted in the nacelle, one to control the lights and the other one the ignition. Provision was made for emergency start should the battery for any 73 reason be discharged. Ignition on-off was controlled by a removable key, which, when rotated anti-clockwise, brought in this emergency start. This had the effect of putting most of the alternator output through the ignition system to provide direct ignition. It would seem the theory was better than the practice for unless the ignition timing and alternator/rotor timing were precisely matched (they seldom were) rough running and mis-firing resulted.

However, the system eventually showed Triumph's faith in it for nearly all motorcycles and cars were subsequently equipped with alternator systems.

Pioneering again, Triumph introduced the AC charging system

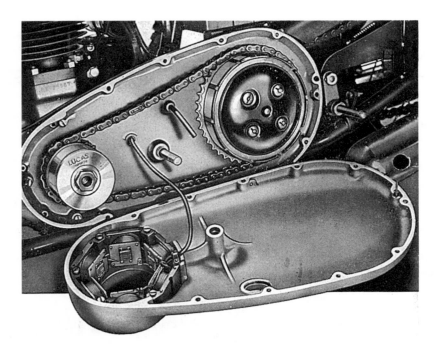

74   The charging unit

Engine

Due to the change from dynamo to alternator the dynamo drive became redundant and new crankcases without this provision were used. A new left hand crankshaft having a parallel section for the alternator rotor mounting was required.

New camshafts with quietening ramps but giving the same valve timing were specified. Where these were used, the crankcase was marked with the spoked wheel sign alongside the engine number. Tappet clearance with these camshafts was 0.010 inch inlet/exhaust with a cold engine. The first engine to be fitted with these camshafts was 37560 on February 16th 1953.

Transmission

New inner and outer primary chaincases were required to house the Lucas alternator.

A new clutch having a built-in shock absorber was fitted. This took the form of a four paddle vane working in eight rubber blocks, giving drive and rebound cushioning. Fitted from 33868 on October 14th 1952.

Inside the shock absorber

Exhaust system

A new left hand exhaust pipe was required having a 'dog leg' bend to clear the new primary chainchase.

Frame

The prop stand footpiece was extended around the exhaust pipe to provide easier application.

The front engine plates reverted to the 1938 pattern with no dynamo cutout.

Toolbox

The toolbox lost its top 'P' clip fitting. As a tidying-up operation the toolbox was now bolted directly to the front half of the rear mudguard.

Rear number plate

A new number plate was required to accommodate the oblong stop and tail lamp.

Electrical
Ignition:
A Lucas DKX2A distributor replaced the magneto.
A Lucas 6V Q6 coil was fitted above the distributor.
Suppressors were now incorporated in the spark plug caps.
Charging systems:
The Lucas RM12 alternator had a 55 watt output. The original MkI system was fitted from 33868 to 35316.

From 35317 on December 12th 1952 a modified MkII system was fitted, essentially simplified wiring.

From 40294 on May 6th 1953, a resistance unit was added. Fitted under the seat, its function was to absorb excess current and prevent wiring failures.

Tail lamp

A new Lucas Diacon plastic stop and tail lamp, part number 53269A, was fitted. Operation was via the rear brake rod through a spring, with the Lucas stop switch being fixed to a plate anchored to the pillion footrest bolt.

The new look tail lamp

Rectifier

A flat two-plate Westinghouse rectifier was housed under the seat, taking the place of the voltage control unit.

Price	£208	3s	4d
Extras			
Spring wheel	£20	8s	11d
Pillion footrests	£1	0s	6d
Pillion seat	£1	12s	0d
Prop stand	£1	12s	0d
Twinseat	£2	4s	9d

1953 Speed Twin
Road Test Impressions

The 1953 Speed Twin tested was equipped with coil ignition and alternator charging. The new system overcame one of the major drawbacks of coil ignition, reliance on battery condition for starting, incorporating as it did an emergency start circuit whereby full generator output was fed direct to the coil when a discharged battery was encountered.

With the absence of dynamo and magneto drive an even quieter engine resulted. Sweetness in all aspects of the performance was an outstanding characteristic. All controls operated with an easy lightness which made the machine a delight to ride in town or on the open road.

The flexibility of the engine was such that within the limits of available performance, cruising speed was dependent solely upon the mood of the rider. One could quite happily go through the gears without exceeding the speed limit in built up areas or whistle up to 70 mph before engaging top gear. One could cruise at 40 to 70 with the same unobtrusive hum from the silencers and no more than a rustle from the engine.

Starting was exemplary, first depression of the kickstarter invariably bringing the engine to life. The air lever mounted under the seat was only required when the engine was started from cold. Piston slap was noticeable when the engine was first started but disappeared when normal running temperatures were reached. New camshafts having quietening ramps contributed largely towards the quietness of the valve gear.

Transmission was above reproach, the new rubber-in-compression clutch shock absorber smoothing out engine snatch. The gearbox was silent in the indirect ratios and changes whether up or down were completely silent provided a slight pause was made when changing between second and third. Gear pedal movement was silky smooth and light and neutral could be engaged from first or second gear.

Comfort was enhanced by the adoption of the excellent Triumph Twinseat although with a heavily clad rider and passenger a little more length to the seat would have been an advantage.

All controls were fully adjustable and no problem was encountered in arranging these to suit the rider's tastes.

Further aids to comfort were provided by the front and rear wheel suspensions. The telescopic forks absorbed road shocks with a soft progressive action, damping was adequate, and bottoming could only be provoked by braking hard on a bumpy surface with a passenger on board. The Spring Wheel eliminated most shocks from the rear though its short travel meant that severe bumps at high speeds were not completely absorbed.

Straight-ahead steering was positive and the steering damper was not required. On bends and corners the Triumph could be heeled over stylishly with every confidence. In keeping with the rest of the machine's performance both brakes were smooth, progressive and powerful in action.

The large sealed beam light unit gave adequate lighting for speeds up to the seventies on straight roads. The speedometer was checked and found to be ten per cent fast at all speeds.

Appreciated was the four gallon fuel tank with its offset filler cap giving an easy visual check of the fuel level. The tank top parcel grid was commented upon favourably and the prop stand could be easily operated with the foot. Add to these features the excellent amaranth red and chromium plate finish, which inspired pride of ownership.

Maximum Speeds

Top Gear (5 to 1)   83 mph 5400 rpm.   Second Gear (8.45 to 1) 60 mph 6570 rpm.
Third Gear (5.95 to 1) 76 mph 5860 rpm.

Measured Quarter Mile		Braking from 30 mph	
Flying start	83.5 mph	Front brake only	37 feet
Standing start	54 mph	Rear brake only	48 feet
		Both brakes	30 feet

Fuel Consumption

Urban	64 mpg
Overall	72 mpg

Model 5T 1954 Speed Twin
Engine Prefix 5T
Engine and Frame Numbers 45578 – 7.10.1953 to 55493 – 8.7.1954
Alterations from 1953

The electrical system introduced in 1953 was improved upon considerable both in appearance and function.

The previous two switches in the nacelle were changed to one double banked combined lighting and ignition switch (Lucas PRS8).

A circular four-plate Sentercel rectifier of 4¹/2 in diameter was specified, replacing the square Westinghouse type. Location was still under the rider's seat.

Wiring was further simplified by the use of a Lucas RM14 alternator.

The appearance of the machine was altered slightly by the use of the barrel-shaped silencers– common to the swinging arm model.

1954 was ostensibly the last year of the rigid or spring wheel Speed Twin but in actuality orders were still being fulfilled in 1955 and the last one of this type was built on June 6th, 1955, Engine and Frame number 68296. Most of these spring wheel 1955 models were the 5TR variant built for institutional use, usually the police.

Engine
The right-hand timing side main bearing was increased in size to 1.125 in x 2.812 in x 0.812 in and changed from a roller bearing to a ball journal on engine numbers 54946 to 54985 only.

The remaining 1954 engines up to 55493 reverted to the previous specification i.e. a roller bearing 1.00 in x 2.50 in x 0.750 in.

Gearbox
No change.

Frame
No change.

Silencers
Barrel-shaped silencers as used on the swinging arm models replaced the parallel tubular pattern.

Electrical
A Lucas PRS8 combined ignition and lighting switch was used.

A 4¹/2 in diameter round Sentercel rectifier was fitted under the seat.

The alternator was updated by the use of a Lucas RM14 assembly

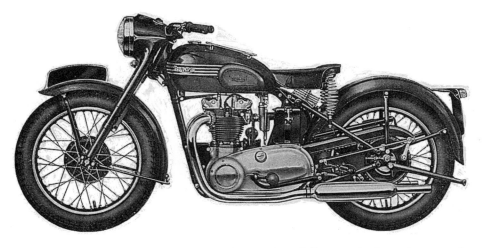

This 1954 view shows the circular rectifier and barrel-shaped silencers – both new items new for the year

Price	£190 16s 0d
Extras	
Spring wheel	£19 4s 0d
Twinseat	£2 2s 0d
Pillion footrests	19s 3d
Prop stand	18s 8d
Pillion Seat	£2 0s 0d

(right) **The new combined ignition and lighting switch**

Two Southend-on-Sea officers enjoy a run in the sun on 1954 Speed Twins. Legshields were a general fitment on police machines

79

Model 5T 1955 Speed Twin
Engine Prefix 5T
Engine and Frame Numbers 55494 – 7.7.1954 to 70196 – 22.7.1955
Alterations from 1954

The visual appearance of this year's Speed Twin was radically changed by the introduction of the swinging arm frame. On reflection this was the first major change in its appearance since 1945 when the telescopic front fork was introduced.

It still vaguely resembled the 1945 model but had now put on a few pounds in weight. With the emphasis on the sports models the Speed Twin was taking an ever increasing background role. True it still had a few faithful followers and one supposes that for the rider who wanted good solid performance with reliability he need look no further.

As in 1953 when the AC generator was first introduced, the Speed Twin model was the first to specify the new Amal Monobloc carburettor. History shows that the new instrument acquitted itself well and all Triumph models (except the 6T) would specify a Monobloc for 1956.

Less visual but just as important was the introduction of a more robust crankshaft having a larger load capacity bearing on the right hand timing side and larger big end journals.

To match the crankshaft new connecting rods were necessary having a larger big end bearing and being generally strengthened all round to cope with the power of the 650 cc T110 model on which the crankshaft assembly had been commonised.

For 1955 the Speed Twin gained swinging arm rear suspension

Engine
The right hand timing side main bearing was increased in size to 1.125 in x 2.812 in x 0.812 in and changed from a roller bearing to a ball journal.

The crankpin size was increased to 1.6235 in/1.6240 in.

The connecting rod big end diameter was increased to 1.6250 in/1.6255 in.

Phillips cross head screws replaced the slotted cheesehead type.

A sludge tube was fitted to the crankshaft from engine number 56811, on August 24th 1954.

Engines with numbers 70076 to 70089 from July 20th 1955 were fitted with a 1956 type crankcase and cylinder barrel.

Carburettor

Amal Monobloc	376/25
Bore	$1^5/16$ in
Main Jet	200
Needle Jet	.1065
Throttle valve	$3^1/2$
Throttle needle	C
Needle Position	3 (middle groove)
Pilot Jet	130

Transmission

Primary chain $1/2$in x .305 in x 70 links.
Secondary chain $5/8$in x $3/8$in x 100 links.

Gearbox

Phillips cross head screws replaced the slotted cheesehead type.

The main gearbox casing now had a top pivot fixing to accommodate the swinging arm frame.

The gearbox inner cover was changed to provide an angled cable adjuster that would clear the gearbox mounting plates.

Primary chaincase

Phillips cross head screws replaced the slotted cheesehead type.

New shorter inner and outer primary cases were needed to accept the swinging arm frame. The inner cover now served as the mounting for the stator assembly, to provide more reliable concentricity between stator and rotor and enabling the air gap between the two to be reduced to 0.008 in.

Frame

A completely new frame was used for the Speed Twin although it had been fitted for a full year to the 1954 Tiger 100 and 110 models. The swinging arm was controlled by Girling suspension units with a length between fixing centres of 12.9 in.

Front forks

A slight modification to improve rigidity was the use of $3/8$ in diameter stanchion pinch bolts to replace the previous $5/16$ in ones.

Mudguards

No change to the front mudguard but the rear was completely new having pressed steel valances spot welded to its sides. The main aim was to disguise the large gap between wheel and mudguard and thereby improve the appearance, especially when the motorcycle was on the centre stand. The valances also provided better weather protection for the rider and passenger during inclement weather.

Wheels

No change was made to the front wheel but the rear dispensed with the old taper roller bearings in favour of ball journal bearings. The quickly detachable wheel used special thin taper bearings in the hub.

Twinseat

This was now a standard fitment and was of the two level type.

Electrical

A new, smaller, Sentercel rectifier of $2^3/4$ in diameter (Lucas type FSX 150 1A) replaced the $4^1/2$ in one.

A new stop/tail lamp of oblong shape with a squared end was fitted. A reflector was built into the lens as a safety feature.

Dimensions		Price	£210 12s 0d
Wheelbase	56 in	**Extras**	
Seat Height	31 in	Prop stand	18s 8d
Ground clearance	5 in	Pillion footrests	19s 3d
Weight	395 lb	QD wheel	£3 12s 0d
Overall length	85¹/₂ in		

A 1955 Speed Twin in police trim for the London Metropolitan Police Force

Model 5T 1956 Speed Twin
Engine Number Prefix 5T
Engine and Frame Numbers
71642 – 15.9.1955 to 82443 – 26.6.1956 then 0602 – 18.7.1956 to 0932 – 22.8.1956
Alterations from 1955

Most of the changes for 1956 were of a minor nature, but one major change that the restorer should be aware of is the use of 650 cc 6T crankcases and a cylinder barrel special to the Speed Twin to accept those crankcases.

This modification applied to all 1956, 1957 and 1958 models right up to the introduction of the unit-construction 5TA model.

Most noticeable visually was the relocation of the pilot light. Up to 1956 this had been located on the fork shrouds just under the headlamp but for 1956 a chrome plated grille occupied this position with the pilot light being placed within the actual sealed beam light unit.

To combat petrol tank failures usually associated with the T100 and T110 sports machines a new rubber-mounted rear bracket was standardised on all twin cylinder models.

Engine

From 72028 of September 23 1955 the inlet camshaft had only one hole, to reduce oil being vented through the breather pipe.

The con-rods were redesigned to use Vandervell shell bearings on the big-end journals.

650 cc dimensions were employed on the cylinder flange and crankcase joint. As a result the outer cylinder fixing holes were increased from 2 in to $2^1/_4$ in centres.

Carburettor

The Monobloc carburettor sealing at the flange joint was improved by the addition of an 'O' ring.

Transmission

New friction material in the form of "Neo-Langite" stick-on pads was used on the clutch friction plates.

Forks

A chrome plated grille replaced the underslung pilot light. The end plug of the hydraulic damper tube was redesigned to prevent bottoming during hard braking.

Frame

Sidecar lugs were incorporated on the main frame and adjustable steering lock stops were fitted to the steering head lug. The top steering stem cup and cone were increased in size and made interchangeable with the bottom ones. As a result the bearings were changed to 40 off $^1/_4$ in ball. A fully rubber-mounted rear tank bracket was fitted.

Petrol tank

A chrome plated centre band was now fitted to cover the centre weld. To miss the centre band on the tank the middle bar of the tank grid was deleted and a two bar grid introduced as a replacement.

Wheels

The painted centres of the wheel rims were deleted, the rims now reverting to a plain chrome finish.

Handlebars

A new type of handlebar was fitted with the threaded hole for the horn push deleted.

Electrical

A new style wiring harness incorporated a 1 mm thick plastic sheath. The pilot light was relocated in the sealed beam reflector. A combined horn and dip switch was mounted on the clutch lever clamp bracket to replace the two separate items used previously.

Price	£217 4s 0d
Extras	
Prop Stand	18s 8d
Pillion footrests	19s 3d
QD rear wheel	£3 12s 0d

TRANSCONTINENTAL SPEED TWIN

This is how the much travelled Speed Twin looked after the Triumph Service Department had worked their deft touches on it.

Ridden overland from India it was a very sorry sight when it arrived at the works main gate. The silencers and exhaust pipes were just about functioning due to great dents and holes, the wheels were far from round with flattened rims and the handlebars and controls were totally scrap. Many other parts had been welded and rewelded, but true to tradition were still performing.

The two travellers names are not committed to history but second from the left is Export Manager A.J. Mathieu and fourth from left is Advertising Manager I. Davies.

Model 5T 1957 Speed Twin
Engine Prefix 5T
Engine and Frame Numbers 01797 – 19.9.1956 to 010253 – 20.8.1957
Alterations from 1956

For 1957 the main visual change was the full-width front hub and the new basket weave petrol tank badges.

The front brake, apart from the use of straight pull spokes, had little else to offer with the added disadvantage of increased weight.

Most of the other changes were of a minor progressive nature with a view to eradicating customer complaints from the previous year. The changes mostly applied to other models in the programme with the Speed Twin benefiting as these changes were applied across the board.

All Speed Twins built for police use have a W suffix to the engine number.

New tank motifs, full-width front brake, relocated coil and extended chainguard denote this as a 1957 model

Engine
No change.

Gearbox
The high gear sleeve bush was extended to protrude into the primary chaincase so ensuring any leakage along the bush would be caught in the primary case. The bush could be fitted retrospectively providing the sliding plate on the inner chaincase was modified to accept the bush.

Transmission
More resilient and oil proof drive and rebound rubbers were fitted to the shock absorber unit.

Front forks
A more robust method of mounting the front wheel spindle comprising split half clamps and $5/16$ in bolts was specified. The loose clips holding the front mudguard centre stay were dispensed with and bottom members with welded-on lugs substituted.

Petrol tank

Basket weave tank badges of chrome plate with an amaranth red background were used. Two horizontal chrome strips, one front and one rear, finished off the embellishment. A new tank with the appropriate screw pommels was required.

Wheels

A 7 in diameter full-width cast iron drum on a steel pressed hub with double butted straight pull spokes was introduced. An alloy anchor plate retained the brake shoes whilst on the opposite side a chrome styling plate was fitted.

The full-width front brake drum

Chainguard

The chainguard remained basically the same but the rear end covering the sprocket was extended to prevent chain lubricant being thrown on to the machine.

Exhaust system

Strengthened exhaust pipe brackets and added silencer brackets improved the method of mounting.

Controls

A new front brake cable was fitted, with the cable adjuster and stop moved to the centre mudguard stay bracket position.

Electrical

The ignition coil was repositioned and fitted above the distributor.

Weight	395 lb
Price	£251 14s 5d

Extras

Prop stand	19s 3d
Pillion footrests	19s 11d
QD rear wheel	£3 14s 5d

Model 5T 1958 Speed Twin
Engine Prefix 5T
Engine and Frame Numbers 011116 – 20.9.1957 to 0200074 – 28.8.1958
Alterations from 1957

1958 saw the introduction of the controversial auto clutch or as Triumph designated it, the Slick Shift. The idea was that gear changes could be achieved without the use of the hand operated clutch lever (quite why anyone wanted to was never determined). All one could say in its favour was that should clutch cable failure occur, the machine could still be ridden until a repair was made. It seemed quite a penalty to offset such an occurrence.

When using the Slick Shift one felt rather ill at ease watching the handlebar clutch lever perform its in and out each time the gearchange was operated. A small point here was that due to this lever movement many clutch lever nipples were lost before the reason became apparent. In consequence a small split pin was introduced to solve the problem.

When the Press tested the Slick Shift one got the impression that they were not very enthusiastic about it with comments such as "unfortunately the booted foot is less sensitive than the rider's hand" and "the revs had to be about right or there was noticeable evidence of strain on the transmission". A final word on this was provided by Bob McIntyre after some miles testing Shell X100 motor oil using a T110. "This thing will maim someone" was his comment although he used somewhat stronger words!

An anti-theft lock was introduced, taking the form of a slot cut in the steering stem which, when the steering was turned to full lock, aligned with a tube in the head lug. Into this could be inserted a lock and key. Strangely, the lock and key were catalogued as an optional extra. A small but very welcome modification was to the oil tank filler cap. This was relocated towards the centre of the machine to obviate the painful contact that could occur with the rider's inside thigh when kick-starting.

Visually, the most obvious change was to the front and rear mudguards. These were now deep-drawn pressings with the side valances in one piece with the mudguard. Prior to this the side valances had been spot welded to the mudguard and rusting could occur at this joint.

1958 was the end of an era. The Speed Twin introduced in 1938 would no longer look the same. Next year's models (1959) would be totally different and the original line would be broken.

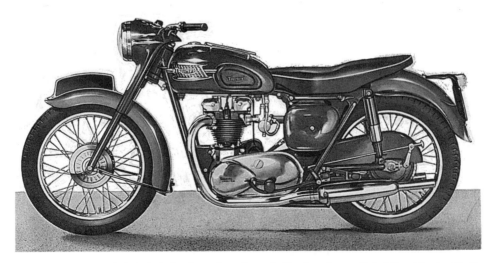

Modifications for 1958 included valanced mudguards front and rear, fluted front brake cover and easy lift centre stand

Engine

To prevent oil transfer between the engine and the primary chaincase the crankcase was modified to accept an oil seal and the engine sprocket boss was ground to suit.

Gearbox

The gearbox was modified to accept the auto clutch or Slick Shift as it was termed. This entailed new gearbox inner and outer covers with the clutch cable stop being transferred from the top of the inner cover to the primary chain adjuster drawbolt. The cable adjuster at the gearbox end was dispensed with. Better oil retention was aimed at by the introduction of a rubber sleeve on the kickstart spindle.

The new end cover on the gearbox houses the "Slick Shift" mechanism

Frame

An anti-theft steering lock was introduced.

Oil Tank

The oil tank filler cap was relocated more to the centre of the machine so preventing fouling during kickstarting.

Front Forks

New mounting lugs for the centre mudguard stay were introduced on the inside of the fork member: A much neater and cleaner appearance was thus achieved.

The front brake cable stop was moved to the bottom of the right-hand fork leg with no adjuster at this point.

The top fork nacelle was modified by passing the brake and clutch cables through small grommets to provide easier routing and operation. The steering damper hole in the nacelle top was also modified by being made larger.

Controls

New clutch and brake cables were fitted, having detachable barrel nipples at the lever ends. The front brake cable was now extended to the bottom of the right-hand lower fork leg, dispensing with the steel tube over its lower run that had been in use since 1945.

Mudguards

Both front and rear mudguards were now manufactured from deep pressings. On the front mudguard the two forward stays were dispensed with and a new centre stay added.

The last pre-unit 1958 Speed Twin to be built as a production batch was 020074 on August 29th 1958 but inexplicably there were a few assembled in 1959 and these were:

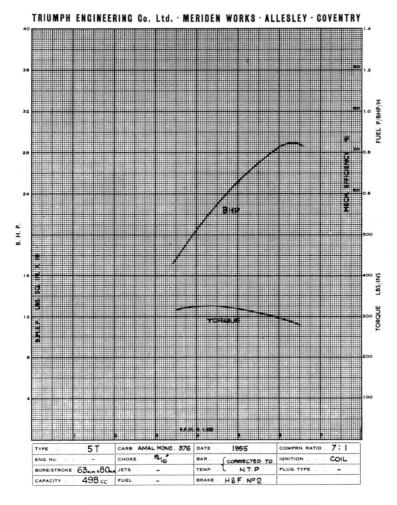

TYPE	5 T	CARB	AMAL MONO. 376	DATE	1955	COMPRN. RATIO	7 : 1
ENG. No.	-	CHOKE	$\frac{5}{16}$	BAR. CORRECTED TO		IGNITION	COIL
BORE/STROKE	63mm x 80mm	JETS	-	TEMP. N.T.P		PLUG. TYPE	-
CAPACITY	498 cc	FUEL	-	BRAKE	H & F. Nº 2		

A typical Speed Twin power and torque graph

Quantity		
1	020376	17.9.1958
24	022663 to 022687	10.12.1958
6	023699 to 023704	6.1.1959
9	023925 to 023933	2.2.1959

It is fairly safe to assume that these machines would closely follow the 1958 specification but may have had 1959 modifications added such as:-

Gearbox oil level indicator incorporated in gearbox inner cover.

Induction hardened gearbox camplate

Front brake cam lever angle changed to give better brake operation.

Price	£253 4s 11d
Extras	
Prop stand	19s 4d
Pillion footrests	£1 0s 0d
Steering lock	13s 4d
QD rear wheel	£3 14s 11d

Senior police officers were invited to inspect a fully-equipped Speed Twin. The legshields and the engine cowling are left and right hand one-piece mouldings. An Avon fairing completes the specification

Safety bars and spot lamps have been added

PART FOUR

Excitement and Demise

The Model 5TA Speed Twin
1959 – 1966

For 1959 a completely new design of Speed Twin was produced. With a capacity of 490 cc it closely followed the existing 348 cc model 21/3TA but had an oversquare bore and stroke.

Based upon the 3TA which had been on sale for some two years prior to the 5TA's introduction one would expect it to have been relatively trouble free and so it proved.

Apart from the colour (the 5TA retained the amaranth red) there was very little in common with its earlier 5T counterprt. With its large valanced front mudguard and total rear enclosure it had little pretence to be regarded as a semi sports model. It was aimed more at the type of motorcyclist who wanted civilised, clean motorcycling, with the minimum of attention.

With its smaller frame and wheels (17in diameter) and its unit-construction engine and gearbox it weighed 35 lb less than its predecessor.

Engine

The ohv valve gear was operated by high camshafts at the front and rear of the cylinder. On the right hand side these camshafts ran direct in the crankcase, having no bushes. On the left hand side they ran in steel-backed thin wall bronze bushes. The crankshaft assembly consisted of two parts. A one-piece forged steel crankshaft over which was threaded a cast iron flywheel was retained to the crankshaft by three high tensile bolts around its periphery. The crankshaft ran on a plain bush on the right hand side and a large ball bearing on the left hand side. End float was determined by locking the crankshaft via the alternator rotor and engine sprocket to the left hand bearing.

The connecting rods were of H section hindiminium alloy bushed at the gudgeon pin end and having steel-backed shell bearings at the big end. Steel caps formed the bottom half of the big end/connecting rod.

The cylinder material was best grade cast iron with the cylinder bores machined directly into it. The cylinder head was of aluminium alloy as were the rocker boxes. The rockers ran direct on steel spindles with no bushes, a method Triumph had used since the early Speed Twin in 1937.

Ignition was supplied by a Lucas distributor located behind the cylinder block and driven by a pair of skew gears from the inlet camshaft.

An Amal 375/75 carburettor of $^7/_8$ in bore supplied the mixture, the choke being of the spring loaded plunger type, on top of the carburettor.

The gearbox was of Triumph manufacture giving four speeds, foot controlled, from the right hand side. The gearbox casting was integral with the engine crankcase. Primary drive was by duplex chain with a slipper tensioner blade to provide adjustment.

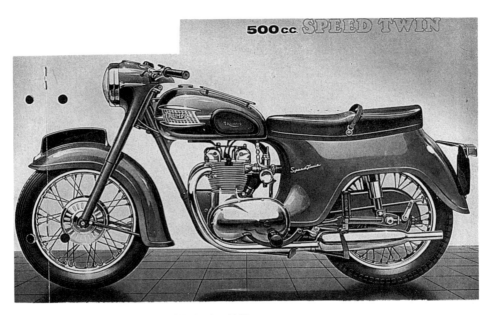

The completely redesigned Speed Twin for 1959

The shock absorber was integral with the clutch comprising a four paddle centre with rubber blocks in compression.

The frame was of the single down tube pattern having only a lower tank rail, the petrol tank forming the upper member when bolted in position.

The front fork was of the telescopic type giving 6 in movement. Hydraulic damping was used to give a hydraulic lock on full depression and extension and so avoid clashing.

The steel petrol tank had a capacity of 3½ gallons. Its filler cap was a Ceandes turn cam action type. Only one petrol tap was fitted, on the left hand side, to provide a main and reserve position.

The oil tank was of welded steel construction being positioned under the side panels on the right hand side of the frame.

The brakes were of Triumph manufacture and of 7 in diameter. The front was within a full-width hub of cast iron with an alloy back plate while the rear was integral with the rear sprocket, also of cast iron but having a steel back plate. Cable operation was used for the front brake and a rod for the rear.

Both wheels were of 17 in diameter, having WM2 chrome steel rims. The front tyre was a 3.25 in ribbed section and the rear a 3.50 Universal, both of Dunlop manufacture.

The front mudguard was a deep valanced type with a flared bottom end. The rear was a simple flat blade under the full rear fairing.

The Twinseat was hinged on the left-hand side under which was a rubber tool tray having individually moulded tool compartments. The seat fixing plunger had a removable knob which gave a degree of security.

The centre stand was fitted with an extension arm which provided a roll-on facility when trodden down. A prop stand was fitted to the left hand lower frame rail.

The exhaust system had two 1½ in diameter pipes terminating into two barrel-shaped silencers with offset entry points.

The electrical system was 6 volt with charging by Lucas alternator via a rectifier. A single 6 volt coil was located on the rear mudguard which supplied the high tension voltage via a distributor.

A 7 in sealed beam headlamp with pilot light provided the front lights, which were controlled by a combined ignition and light (Lucas PRS8) switch. An ammeter, like the ignition switch, was housed in the nacelle top. The horn was located in the nacelle housing and operated by a combined push and dip switch on the clutch lever.

Controls

The handlebars were of 1 in diameter with a Triumph twistgrip and both clutch and brake levers were fitted with knurled hand adjusters.

A 120 mph Smiths speedometer with a plain dial was fitted, being driven from the rear wheel via a speedometer gearbox.

The finish was in amaranth red on all painted parts except the steering damper knob, pillion footrests, number plates and front hub.

Tools

The tools were housed in a wide rubber tray above the rear mudguard. Each tool had its shape formed in the rubber so it was easy to see if the tool kit was complete.

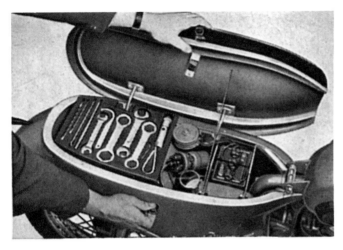

A tool tray with appropriately-shaped tool holders

1959 model 5TA Speed Twin
Technical details

Engine

Bore	69 mm (2.716 in)
Stroke	65.5 mm (2.578 in)
Capacity	490 cc (30 cu in)
bhp	27 at 6500
Compression ratio	7.0:1

Cylinder Head

Material	Aluminium alloy
Valve seat angle	45°
Valve seat width	
Inlet	0.050/0.060 in
Exhaust	0.060/0.080 in
Valve guide bore	0.4980/0.4985 in

93

Valves
Stem diameter
    Inlet   0.3095/0.3100 in
    Exhaust   0.3090/0.3095 in
Head diameter
    Inlet $1^{7}/_{16}$in
    Exhaust $1^{5}/_{16}$ in

Valve Guides
Material   Chilled cast iron
Bore diameter   0.312/0.313 in
Outside diameter   0.5005/0.5100 in
Length
    Inlet   1.750 in
    Exhaust   1.750 in

Valve Springs
Free length nominal
    Inner $1^{1}/_{2} \pm {}^{1}/_{16}$ in
    Outer $1 {}^{21}/_{32} \pm {}^{1}/_{16}$ in
Fitted load   63 lb

Cam Followers
Foot radius   0.750 in
Stem diameter   0.311/0.3115 in
Overall length nominal   2.775 in

Valve Clearances – Cold
Inlet and exhaust   0.010 in

Valve Timing

IVO	$26^{1}/_{2}°$	BTDC	
IVC	$69^{1}/_{2}°$	ABDC	
EVO	$61^{1}/_{2}°$	BBDC	0.020 in clearance for checking timing
EVC	$35^{1}/_{2}°$	ATDC	

Push Rods
Material   Solid aluminium alloy with end caps at top only
Overall length   4.820/4.845 in

Rockers
Bore diameter   0.4375/0.4380 in
Spindle diameter   0.4355/0.4360 in

Camshafts and Bearings
Journal Diameter
    Left hand   0.8100/0.8105 in
    Right hand   1.4355/1.436 in
    End float   0.013/0.020 in
    Lobe height   1.047/1.055 in

Bush Diameter
    Left hand bore   0.8125/0.8135 in
    Left hand outer length
        LH inlet   1.094/1.0114 in
        LH exhaust   0.922/0.942 in
    RH housing diameter   1.437/1.4375 in

Cylinder Barrel
Material	Cast iron
Cylinder bore diameter	2.716/2.7165 in
Max. tolerable wear	0.007 in
Tappet guide bore diameter	0.9985/0.9990 in

Tappet Block
Outer diameter	0.9995/1.000 in
Tappet bore diameter	0.312/0.3125 in

Piston Rings

Ring Gap in Cylinder Bore
Compression ring	0.010/0.014 in
Scraper ring	0.010/0.014 in

Ring Thickness
Compression ring	0.0615/0.625 in
Scraper ring	0.124/0.125 in

Clearance in Piston Groove
Compression ring	0.001/0.003 in
Scraper ring	0.001/0.0025 in

Pistons
Clearance in cylinder at maximum diameter (90° to gudgeon pin)	0.003/0.0045 in
Gudgeon pin diameter	0.6882/0.6886 in

Connecting Rods
Small end bush outer diameter	0.782/0.783 in
Small end bush length	0.890/0.910 in
Small end diameter fitted	0.6905/0.6910 in
Big end diameter	1.4385/1.4390 in
Side clearance (fitted)	0.008/0.012 in
Length between centres	5.311/5.313 in
Bearing big end shell	Vandervell

Crankshaft
Crankpin diameter	1.4375/1.4380 in

Main Bearing Journals
Diameter	1.8135/1.8140 in
Drive side	1.1805/1.1808 in
Timing side	1.4375/1.4380 in
Crankshaft end float	Nil with rotor nut tightened
Balance factor	52%

Crankshaft Bearings
Drive side ball race	72 x 30 x 19 mm
Timing side bush bore	1.4385/1.4390 in
Time side bush outer	1.8115/1.8120 in
Bearing type LH	Ball race
Bearing type RH	Vandervell VP3 bush

Oil Pump
Feed plunger diameter	0.3744/0.3747 in
Scavenge plunger diameter	0.4869/0.4872 in
Feed bore	0.3748/0.3753 in
Scavenge bore	0.4873/0.4878 in

Carburettor

Type	375/3 Amal monobloc
Bore	$7/8$ in
Main jet	160
Needle jet	.105
Needle	B
Needle position	3
Throttle valve	375/3
Pilot jet	25

Ignition

Timing	$1/64$ in BTC fully retarded
Distributor type	Lucas 18D2 clockwise
Advance range (distrib)	15° (30° crankshaft)
Points gap	0.012 in

Spark Plug

	N5 Champion
Plug gap	0.020 in
Thread size	14 mm
Reach	$3/4$ in

Clutch

Friction plates	4
Plain plates	5
Pressure springs	4
Spring free length	1.400/1.500 in
Bearing rollers	20
Bearing size	
Diameter	0.2495/0.250 in
Length	0.231/0.236 in
Hub bearing diameter	1.3733/1.3743 in
Sprocket bore diameter	1.8745/1.8755 in
Clutch rod diameter	$3/16$ in
Clutch rod length	9.562/9.567 in
Clutch plate segment thickness	$3/32$ in

Kickstart Mechanism

Kickstart spindle diameter	1.060/1.0605 in
Kickstart bore diameter	1.062/1.0625 in

Gearchange Mechanism

Quadrant plunger diameter	0.3402/0.3412 in
Plunger bore diameter	0.3427/0.3437 in
Plunger spring No. of coils	16
Plunger spring free length	$1 1/16$ in

Footchange Spindle

Diameter RH	0.621/0.6215 in
Bush diameter RH	0.623/0.624 in

Quadrant Springs

Free length	$1 7/8$ in
No. of coils	18

Camplate Plunger

Plunger diameter	0.4360/0.4365 in

Housing bore	0.4375/0.4380 in
Spring length	$2^{1}/_{2}$ in
No. of coils	22

Mainshaft

Bearing LH	30 x 62 x 16 mm BALL
Bearing RH	17 x 47 x 14 mm BALL
Mainshaft diameter LH	0.7495/0.750 in
Mainshaft sleeve bush	
Bore diameter	0.7520/0.7530 in
Outside diameter	0.910/0.912 in
Length O/A	$2^{19}/_{32}$ in

Layshaft

Bearing diameter LH	0.6845/0.6850 in
Bearing diameter RH	0.6870/0.6875 in
Bush bore LH	0.6865/0.6885 in
Bush outside diameter LH	0.8755/0.8760 in
Bush bore RH	0.689/0.690 in
Bush outside diameter RH	0.8125/0.8130 in

Number of teeth on pinions

Layshaft		Mainshaft
18T	4th	26T
23T	3rd	28T
28T	2nd	23T
32T	1st	19T

Sprockets

	Solo
Engine	26
Clutch	58
Gearbox	19
Rear wheel	43

Gear Ratios Internal

4th	1.00
3rd	1.19
2nd	1.76
1st	2.43

Overall Ratios

4th	5.05
3rd	6.00
2nd	8.9
1st	12.3

rpm at 10mph top gear 720

Chains

Primary endless	$^{3}/_{8}$ in x $^{1}/_{4}$ in x 78 link duplex
Secondary	$^{5}/_{8}$ in x $^{3}/_{8}$ in x 102 link

Frame

Steering head bearings	
Top	24 off $^{3}/_{16}$ in dia. ball
Bottom	24 off $^{3}/_{16}$ in dia. ball

Swinging arm pivot
Bush bore	0.8745/0.8750 in
Spindle diameter	0.8735/0.8740 in
Spindle housing (frame)	0.8725/0.8730 in
Maximum side play	0.015 in

Frame Head Angle   67°

Rear Suspension
Unit type	Girling SB4
Length between centres	$11^3/8$ in
Spring rate	145 lb colour blue/yellow
Spring free length	$8^3/16$ in

Front Fork
Stanchion diameter	1.3025/1.3030 in
Top bush inner diameter	1.3065/1.3075 in
Top bush outer diameter	1.498/1.499 in
Top bush o/a length	0.995/1.005 in
Bottom bush inner diameter	1.2485/1.2495 in
Bottom bush outer diameter	1.4935/1.4945 in
Bottom bush o/a length	0.870/0.875 in
Fork leg bore	1.498/1.500 in
Spring free length	$17^3/4$ in
Wire diameter	0.160 in

Wheels
Rim size front and rear	WM2 x 17 in

A 1959 sidecar-kitted frame

Tyres

Front	3.25 in x 17 in Dunlop ribbed
Rear	3.50 in x 17 in Dunlop Universal
Pressures front and rear	20 psi

Wheel Bearings

Front	20 x 47 x 14 mm ball journal
Rear standard	20 x 47 x 14 mm ball journal
Rear quickly detachable	$3/4$ in x $1^{27}/32$ in x $9/16$ in
	Timkin taper roller

Spokes

Front	40 off butted 8/10 gauge o/a length $5^1/16$ in straight
Rear	20 off butted 8/10 gauge o/a length $7^1/8$ in 110°
	20 off butted 8/10 gauge o/a length $7^1/8$ in 90°

Wheel Offset

Front

Dimension from drum edge to centre of rim	$1^1/2$ in

Rear

Dimension from outer edge of sprocket to centre of rim	$3^5/32$ in

Electrical

Alternator	Lucas RM 13/5
Voltage	6 volt
Earth	Positive
Battery	Lucas 6 volt PUZ7E-11
Horn	Lucas type HF 1441
Headlamp	Lucas 7 in pre focus
Tail lamp	Lucas 564
Bulb main	6 v 30/24 W
Bulb pilot	6 v 3 W
Bulb speed	6 v 3 W
Bulb tail/stop	6 v 6/18 W
Coil	Lucas 6 v MA6
Distributor	Lucas 18D2 clockwise
Rectifier	Lucas FSX 18498
Stop switch	Lucas 6SA (D shape)

Dimensions

Wheelbase	$52^3/4$ in
O/A length	81 in
O/A width	26 in
Seat height	$29^1/4$ in
Weight	350 lb
Ground clearance	5 in

Lubrication

Engine

Summer	SAE 40-50
Winter	SAE 20-30
Gearbox	EP 90
Primary case	SAE 20

99

	Telescopic fork
Summer	SAE 30
Winter	SAE 20

Capacities

Fuel tank	3$^{1}/_{2}$ Imp gall (16 litre)
Oil tank	5 Imp pint (2.8 litre)
Gearbox	$^{2}/_{3}$ Imp pint (375 cc)
Primary case	$^{1}/_{2}$ Imp pint (300 cc)
Telescopic fork	$^{1}/_{4}$ Imp pint (150 cc)

Torque Settings Model 5TA

	lb. ft
Flywheel bolts	33
Connecting rod bolt nuts	26
Cylinder head bolts	18
Kickstart ratchet pinion nut	40
Clutch centre nut	50
Rotor fixing nut	50
Stator fixing nuts	10
Stanchion pinch bolt nuts	25
Gearbox sprocket nut	80
Fork top nuts	80
Camshaft pinion nuts	50
Crankshaft pinion nut	50

Left Hand Threads

Camshaft pinion nuts

1959 Model 5TA Speed Twin
Engine Prefix 5TA
Engine and Frame Numbers H5785 – 25.9.1958 to H11032 – 21.8.1959
Alterations during 1959

Engine
Taper faced compression rings were fitted to pistons from H7116 on December 2nd 1958

Price   £237 12s 0d

Extras

Prop stand	18s 9d
Pillion footrests	19s 4d
QD wheel	£3 12s 5d

1959 Speed Twin
Road Test Impressions

The new Speed Twin with unit construction engine/gearbox assembly was to all intents and purposes identical to the already established 350 cc model Twenty One. Typically Triumph, it has all the attributes one has come to expect from this manufacturer. It was a machine combining the weight of a lightish three-fifty with true five-hundred performance.

Its style may be rather unorthodox when compared with previous Speed Twins but with its sleek lines and partial enclosure it could be thoroughly cleaned in 10-15 minutes with a bucket of water, sponge and wash leather, a point which will be appreciated by the majority of riders.

Just as the first Speed Twin stirred pulses so beyond doubt will the new 5TA excite comment the world over with its square (69 x 65.5 mm) bore and stroke giving a short engine, the gearbox being integral. No five hundred could be more compact. Compactness is a feature of the whole machine. Wheel diameter is 17 in., saddle height $28^{1}/2$ in., wheelbase 52 in. and the total weight 350 lb.

All the controls are fully adjustable with knurled cable adjusters integral with the front brake and clutch control levers. The combined horn button and dip switch is positioned conveniently close to the left handlebar grip.

On the open road at 60 to 65 mph only a muted drone with no mechanical noise was detectable. Acceleration was clean and impressive yet the engine was perfectly happy in top gear at 25 mph. At the other end of the scale 85 mph was comfortably clocked. The unit was leak free except for a slight seep at the oil pressure indicator button.

Starting was faultless. Full choke operated by a spring loaded plunger atop of the carburettor was required when cold but when warm the unit responded to a gentle prod from the kickstart. The ease of starting no doubt was aided by the coil ignition system used.

The transmission worked well but if held in third gear one becomes conscious of gearbox whine. All indirect gears were noisy by Triumph standards but third was especially so. The gear pedal movement was light with slightly more travel than previously and as before, really silent changes required a slight pause in pedal travel. Downward changes could be made just as fast as the controls could be operated. As was usual with Triumphs, the clutch needed freeing by depressing the kickstart pedal with the clutch disengaged to ensure quiet bottom gear engagement.

The Speed Twin's steering was characteristically light to the point that on greasy surfaces it could be a shade too light to give a truly positive feeling. Straight-ahead steering however was true and negotiating sharpish corners a delight. There appeared no limit to the angle to which the machine could be heeled over.

Long, sweeping bends could be treated as if they did not exist. On bumpy surfaces the suspension gave the impression that the spring poundage could be reduced both fore and aft.

Brakes worked well, the centre stand was exemplary with its roll-on tread down lever requiring no effort on the part of the rider. The prop stand held the machine steady, even on cambers, and could easily be operated by the foot due to the extended lever.

Finally, mudguarding scored 99 out of 100 for its efficiency.

Maximum Speeds

Top Gear (4.8 to 1)	87 mph.
Third Gear (5.62 to 1)	77 mph.
Second Gear (8.35 to 1)	54 mph.

Fuel Consumption

Urban	62 mpg
Overall	75 mpg

Braking from 30 mph

Both brakes	29 ft 6 in.

1960 Model 5TA Speed Twin
Engine Prefix 5TA
Engine and Frame Numbers H11962–8.10.1959 to H18626–1.9.1960
Alterations from 1959

Engine
The main bearing bush housing on the right hand side was retained by a locking plate and screw to prevent endways movement from H12014 on October 10th 1959.

Gearbox
No change.

Transmission
A primary chain adjuster was introduced at H13115 on December 3rd 1959. The rear sprocket size was reduced to 43 tooth from 46. The gear ratios were changed accordingly to 5.33, 6.32, 9.37, 12.96 from H11962 on October 8th 1959.

Finish
The traditional Speed Twin amaranth red was abandoned after 22 consecutive years for a brighter red. This was from H11692 on October 8th 1959.

Price	£227 19s 8d

Extras

Prop stand	18s 9d
Pillion footrests	19s 4d
QD rear wheel	£3 12s 5d

Works photo of a 1960 Speed Twin

1962 Model 5TA Speed Twin
Engine Prefix 5TA
Engine and Frame Numbers H25904 – 26.9.1961 to H29727 – 24.9.1962
Alterations from 1961

There were few alterations to the 1962 season's models. Those made were aimed at eliminating customer complaints and reducing the cost to the company.

Engine
Modified head bolts having extended hexagon portions for easier spanner application were fitted from H29151 on June 30th 1962.

Gearbox
Clutch cable replacement could now be made without removing the gearbox outer cover as previously. The cable was attached to a spoke and a threaded thimble housed in a sleeve screwed into the outer cover. The change was made from H25904 on September 26th 1961.

Front Fork
The steering damper assembly was deleted as a cost reduction and the hole in the nacelle top plugged by a rubber grommet from H25904 on September 26th 1961.

Exhaust System
A siamese downswept right hand exhaust system with single barrel-shaped silencer having a concentric entry for the exhaust pipe was fitted from H25904 on September 26th 1961.

Electrical
The sheath covering the distributor and high tension leads was deleted. A Lucas 8H electric horn was fitted and the alternator was changed to a Lucas RM19 from H25904 on September 26th 1961.

Finish
The red finish introduced for 1960 was changed slightly and was now described by Triumph as ruby red.

Price £253 19s 4d

Extras
Prop stand	£1 2s 9d
Pillion footrests	£1 2s 1d
QD rear wheel	£4 2s 10d

(Facing page)
Policemen collect their new mounts from the factory – spring 1961

A works photo of a 1962 show model. The siamesed exhaust system is just visible

1963 Model 5TA Speed Twin
Engine Prefix 5TA
Engine and Frame Numbers H30289 – 1.11.1962 to H32361 – 1.8.1963
Alterations from 1962

Engine
Due to the persistent loss of rocker box inspection caps a retaining spring clip was introduced, fitting under the rocker box fixing nuts and bearing on the milled edge of the inspection cap. The clips were fitted from H32118 on July 10th 1963.

Transmission
A new three-vane shock absorber unit in the clutch centre gave improved movement and smoother cushioning effect. With this new shock absorber came a redesigned clutch with the object of reducing low speed rattle. The clutch load was taken directly on the sprocket face by a thrust washer located between the sprocket and clutch hub. The rear chain was lengthened to 102 link.

Front Fork
New oil seals having larger sealing areas were fitted from H30289 to give better oil retention.

Chainguard
Minor modifications were made to the rear chainguard whereby two $^3/_6$ in holes were pierced to provide a mounting for the repositioned stop lamp switch.

Wheels

Grease retaining washers were fitted inboard of the hub bearings on both front and rear wheels. The rear wheel brake drum/sprocket-to-hub nuts were changed to self lock and the lock tab washers deleted. The rear wheel spokes received minor alterations and now comprised

    20 off left hand side 8/10G x $7^1/8$ in x 90°
    20 off right hand side 8/10G $7^3/8$ in x 90°

Exhaust system

The exhaust system reverted back to the 1961 type with two separate left and right hand pipes and silencers.

Electrical

A miniature round Lucas 2DS 506 silicon rectifier was fitted from H30289. A pull-type Lucas 31383 stop switch was mounted on the rear chainguard and operated through a spring attached to the rear brake rod was fitted. It replaced the 'D' type 6SA.

Finish

Cherry red was now the official colour for this year's Speed Twin.

Price	£274 4s 0d

Extras

Prop stand	£1 4s 8d
Pillion footrests	£1 4s 0d
QD rear wheel	£4 9s 5d

Little change for the 1963 Speed Twin

The 1964 Speed Twin was visually different from the 1963 model for not only had it lost its red finish but also the full rear enclosure.

Another noticeable change was the use of coil ignition activated by twin contact breakers driven off the exhaust camshaft and housed in the timing cover.

Less obvious at first glance was the new front fork with external springs, and smaller diameter handlebars with new control levers and twistgrip. These later changes were a first for the Speed Twin as all telescopic forks since 1943 had featured internal springs and the Triumph manufactured twistgrip had been a well-recognised trade mark dating back to 1937.

Engine

New crankcases having provision for the contact breaker lead to pass through them were fitted. A threaded plug filled the hole left by the now obsolete distributor.

A new exhaust camshaft having an internal taper on the drive end was fitted to accommodate the 4CA Lucas auto advance unit.

A new timing cover was specified having a housing adjacent to the end of the exhaust camshaft to carry the 4CA twin contact breaker and condenser assemblies.

Push rod cover tube sealing was improved by the use of square section sealing rings top and bottom. This necessitated the use of new cover tubes and tappet blocks.

Gearbox

The selector camplate was induction hardened to give better wearing properties adjacent to the plunger track. Additionally, a bridging strap was incorporated, spanning the selector slots, to prevent these widening in use.

The clutch operation was improved by the use of a lift mechanism similar to that fitted on the larger Triumph Twins. It comprised two steel pressings with three indents in each having three steel $3/8$ in ball bearings interposed between them. Rotation of the plate caused the bearings to ride up the indents and impart movement to the push rod. Advantages were a lighter clutch action and better wearing properties, improvements over the quick thread mechanism it replaced.

Front Fork

The fork was completely redesigned and featured external springs of $8^3/4$ in length x 0.192 in wire diameter. Larger seal holders were fitted having a seal of 1.875 in x 0.435 in x 1.235 in. The fork sliders contained a short taper oil restrictor to provide damping and a hydraulic stop, on full bump position. New separate spring covers and headlamp nacelle covers completed the changes.

Handlebars

These were shaped as previously but the diameter was reduced from 1 in to $7/8$ in. The U bolt fixings and the top fork yoke were left at 1 in diameter and four packing pieces added to take up the difference.

Controls

The reduced handlebar diameter meant the fitting of new clutch and brake lever assemblies. They not only differed in the fitting diameter but to aid cable removal the actual clamp bracket was slotted as was the adjuster and lock ring. Fixed barrel cable nipples were reintroduced, replacing the loose barrel nipples required with the previous non-slotted clamp brackets. A standard Amal twistgrip and shorter Amal handlebar grips replaced the previous Triumph ones.

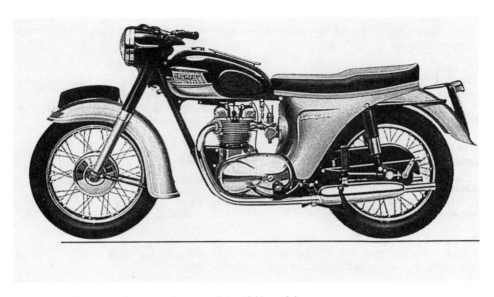

Abbreviated rear panels were a feature of the 1964 model

The new clutch operating mechanism

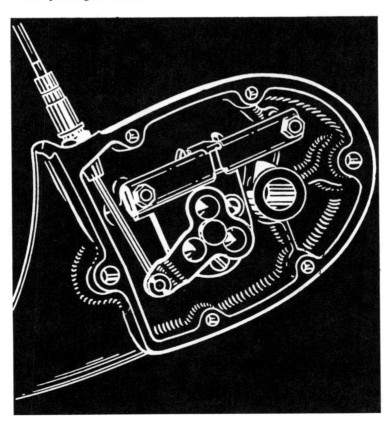

Petrol Tank

A revised petrol tank was fitted, with recesses either side of the centre tunnel to accommodate the two ignition coils.

Oil Tank

This item was now rubber-mounted to prevent fatigue failure at the mounting brackets. This modification brought the Speed Twin into line with the other twin cylinder models.

A separate oil drain plug was incorporated to assist servicing. Prior to this the feed pipe and filter had to be removed to allow drainage, resulting in a messy operation.

Side Panels

Small quarter panels replaced the full enclosure previously fitted.

Rear Mudguard

With the above small panels a full rear mudguard was reintroduced. This was fitted with a wrap-round rear stay and a new rear number plate compatible with the mudguard.

Air Filter

A small round air filter having a perforated chrome plated band was fitted directly on to the carburettor, the side panels being shaped to accommodate it.

Tool Tray

The tool tray was redesigned and relocated to fit on to the rear mudguard just to the rear of the battery.

Speedometer

A Smiths magnetic SSM5002/00 speedometer was fitted, replacing the Smiths Chronometric SC 3304/11 instrument used previously.

Electrical

The ignition system was greatly improved by the use of a Lucas 4CA twin contact breaker and automatic advance assembly. Twin Lucas MA6 6 volt coils were fitted on the bottom frame rail and recesses in the petrol tank housed them.

The single Lucas PRS8 combined ignition and light switch gave way for the use of separate Lucas 88SA light and ignition switches. These switches were of the plug and socket type and were prone to unplug until a small steel pressing and an elastic band were fitted as retainers.

A smaller diameter Lucas type 2AR ammeter was fitted as was a Lucas 8H horn.

A Lucas MLZ8E battery was used for this season bringing the Speed Twin into line with the other models. This replaced the previously used Lucas PUZ7E-11 battery.

Finish:- Silver and black.

Petrol tank: Gloss black top half and around the knee grips with silver sheen lower half. A gold line separated the two colours. The badge background was gold as was the Triumph lettering. The background of the Triumph lettering was black.

Mudguards: Silver sheen

Rear panels: Silver sheen

Front forks: Nacelle top, lower nacelle covers and spring covers were gloss black with the lower fork sliders Silver sheen.

All other painted parts were finished in gloss black.

Price	£283 1s 5d

Extras

Prop stand	£1 6s 0d
Pillion footrests	£1 5s 0d
Q.D. rear wheel	£4 14s 1d

Redesigned oil sealing on the push rod cover tubes

1965 Model 5TA Speed Twin
Engine Prefix 5TA
Engine and Frame Numbers H36615 – 29.9.1964 to H39838 – 1.6.1965
Alterations from 1964

Engine
The flywheel periphery was drilled to accept a service tool to locate TDC and also the 38° BTDC firing point.
   The oil pressure release valve tell-tale button was deleted and replaced by a plain dome nut.

Frame/Petrol Tank
A new petrol tank was fitted, rubber mounted at its four corners. The frame now had a bolt-in top rail to replace the former fuel tank that had doubled-up as a stressed member. If used as a kit it could be fitted retrospectively.

Front Fork
A revised design was fitted with shorter bottom sliders and longer $9^3/4$ in springs to give greater rider comfort.
   The bottom sliders were made from one piece extrusions. Previously they had comprised tubes brazed on to forgings. The new replacements gave a neater appearance and were cheaper to produce.

Front Mudguard
A semi-sports blade with bolt on front stays replaced the large valanced pattern used previously.

Rear Number Plate
The rear number plate was extended to accommodate the seven digit registration figures now in use.   111

A sportier front mudguard for 1965

When duty calls – a WD Speed Twin known at the factory as a T50WD. Only seventeen were built. Most obvious departures from standard were a petrol tank with snorkel tube to provide clean air, full rear chain enclosure and a 1950s front brake assembly

Front Number Plate
The front number plate lost its chrome-plated surround reverting to a plain steel blade last used on the Speed Twin in 1938.

Price £283 1s 9d

Extras

Prop stand	£1 6s 0d
Pillion footrests	£1 5s 0d
Q.D. rear wheel	£4 14s 1d

1966 Model 5TA Speed Twin
Engine Prefix 5TA
Engine and Frame Numbers H42227 – 8.9.1965 to H46431 – 25.5.1966
Alterations from 1965

1966 was the final year of the Speed Twin, the last being built on May 25th 1966.

Engine
A sports camshaft was fitted with inlet 3134 form and exhaust 3325 form. The 3134 camshaft height from base circle was 1.120 in/1.128 in and the 3325 camshaft height from base circle 1.102 in/1.110 in.

Camshaft Timing

IVO	34°	BTDC	
IVC	55°	ABDC	checked with 0.020 in tappet clearance
EVO	48°	BBDC	
EVC	27°	ATDC	

Tappet Clearance (cold engine)

Inlet	0.002 in
Exhaust	0.004 in

Gearbox
The gearbox sprocket was reduced by one tooth to 19T.

Transmission
The clutch push rod adjuster was increased in diameter to $3/8$ in from $1/4$ in. This change necessitated a new pressure plate having a larger inserted nut.

Frame
The previously bolt-on top tube was now made a permanent feature by being welded in. It was used from H42227.

Oil Tank
The oil tank was increased in capacity to 6 pints and fitted with an adjustable rear chain oiler. This took the form of a spring-retained screw positioned just inside the oil tank filler neck. A pipe was then routed down the left side terminating at the brake torque stay. A small extension pipe directed oil onto the rear chain.

Petrol Tank
New "bird wing" style tank motifs were used from H42227 replacing the basket weave pattern.

Not the ultimate but certainly the last Speed Twin was this 1966 model

The built-in steering lock

Side Panels

Only one side panel was used and this was a reverse copy of the oil tank pressing, fitted on the left hand side covering the battery.

Handlebars

White rubber fluted grips were fitted from H42227.

Front Wheel

A change in wheel size to WM2 x 18 in required a new tyre. A Dunlop 3.25 in x 18 in ribbed was the size chosen. New spokes were also required, 40 off 8/10G x $5^5/8$ in.

Rear Wheel

A change in wheel size to WM2 x 18 in required a new tyre, a Dunlop Universal 3.50 in x 18 in being the size chosen. New spokes were also required, 20 off 8/10G x $7^9/16$ in x 90°, 20 off 8/10G x $7^7/8$ in x 90° were the sizes for both the standard and quickly detachable wheels.

The standard wheel sprocket reverted to the pre-1952 type comprising a 46 tooth steel sprocket ring bolted to the cast iron brake drum by eight bolts. The sprocket and brake drum remained integral and of cast iron in the case of the quickly detachable wheel.

Electrical

The charging system was now 12 volt, diode controlled. The battery was a single Lucas PUZ5A. The diode was mounted on an aluminium plate bolted to the battery carrier.

The stop lamp switch remained as previously, but its operation differed in so far as the spring connection was dropped in favour of a fixed metal bracket fitted to the brake rod with the switch lever abutting against it.

Bulbs

12 volt	
Headlamp	50/40W LH dip pre-focus
Pilot	4W MCC
Tail lamp/stop	6/21W offset pin
Speedometer	3W MES

Coils

Lucas MA12	12 volt

Horn

Lucas 8H 12 Volt
Fuse 35 amp

Price

£283 1s 5d

Extras

Prop Stand	£1	6s 0d
Pillion Footrest	£1	5s 0d
D Rear Wheel	£4	14s 1d

Unfortunately it cannot be said that 1966 was a vintage year. One look at what was offered as a Speed Twin will be sufficient for most to agree it was not much more than a collection of parts borrowed from other models in the range.

It would seem on the one hand the company did not want to continue production of the Speed Twin but on the other hand, because of its long pedigree and illustrious past, they did not want to kill it off either.

Looking back at its history one sees it as emerging as a motorcycle with huge potential in 1938, carrying the firm through in the late forties along with its sister model, the Tiger 100, then losing ground a little when the Thunderbird was released in the early 1950s and most definitely being relegated to the back row in the mid-1950s when the Tiger 110 was the most sporty motorcycle one could possess.

It must have given Triumph quite a lift to see when tested in 1938 that the Speed Twin was the fastest 500cc motorcycle over the flying quarter mile and second fastest over the standing quarter mile, losing out by only 0.2mph to a Rudge Ulster.

In 1939 the road tests showed it was bettered only by its sister machine, the Tiger 100, in the 500cc class. This time it beat the Rudge Ulster by 0.19mph over the flying quarter mile and by 2.13mph over the standing quarter. When one considers that the tests included the Rudge, Norton, BSA and Velocette sports models of the day, the Speed Twin results can be even more appreciated.

PERFORMANCE FIGURES: 500 cc

Make	Model	Flying 1/4 mile	Standing 1/4 mile	Year
Norton	ES2	81.8 mph	49.4 mph	1938
Rudge	Special	75.0	45.68	"
Rudge	Ulster	89.1	51.72	"
Triumph	5T	91.8	51.70	"
Matchless		84.0	–	"
HRD	Comet	90.0	48.9	"
BSA	Gold Star	89.0	51.4	"
AJS	Model 18	81.8	50.5	"
Norton	ES2	81.81	50.56	1939
Norton	18	81.08	50.56	"
OEC		80.6	47.40	"
Rudge	Ulster	89.0	50.50	"
Triumph	T100	95.74	56.96	"
Triumph	5T	89.19	52.63	"
Velocette	MSS	83.72	48.65	"
Norton	International	94.71	56.01	1947
Ariel	Red Hunter	86.53	52.32	"
Moto Guzzi		85.7	51.7	1950

In the late 1950s the Speed Twin was again in the limelight with its full skirted rear panels but fashion changed and Triumph's markets were in the United States where sports motorcycles were in demand. I am led to believe that Edward Turner was very disappointed at the turn of events (although not with the sales) as he would have liked to see at a more civilised two wheeled form of transport, perhaps a 650 cc scooter, but it was not to be.

With fashion changing, the Speed Twin found itself with a rapidly diminishing market. 500 cc was hardly the model to buy for riding to work – this function was admirably filled by the 200 cc Triumph Cub, and as said earlier, the Speed Twin had no sporting pretensions so it had really come to the end of the line.

SPEED TWIN COLOURS
1938-1966

	1938-'49	1950	1951-'58	1959	1960-'62	1963	1964-'66
Petrol Tank	Chrome with Amaranth red top & side panels twin gold lining	Amaranth red	Amaranth red chrome styling styling bands with amaranth red background	Amaranth red	Ruby red	Cherry red	Black & silver sheen & gold lining
Frame	1938-1959 Amaranth red	1960-1962 Ruby red	1963 Cherry red	1964-1966 Black			
Mudguards	1938-1959 Amaranth red. Gold lining	1960-1962 Ruby red	1963 Cherry red	1964-1966 Silver sheen			
Rear Panels	1959 Amaranth red	1960-1962 Ruby red	1963 Cherry red	1964-1966 Silver sheen			
Front Forks	1959 Amaranth red	1960-1962 Ruby red	1963 Cherry red	1964-1966 Black nacelle upper & lower. Silver sheen btm members			

	1938-1951	1952	1953-1955	1956-1966
Wheel Rims	Chrome with amaranth red. Centres gold lined	Silver sheen amaranth red. Centres gold lined	As 1938/51	All chrome rims
Steering damper knob	1938-1947 Black Bakelite self colour	1948-1961 Gloss black	1962-1966 Non fitted	
Pillion footrests	1938-1966 Gloss black			
Stand springs	1939-1966 Gloss black			
Rear suspension units	1955-1958 Amaranth red and chrome	1960-1962 Ruby red and chrome	1963 Cherry red and chrome	1964-1966 Black and chrome
Front brake drum and hub	1938-1959 Amaranth red	1960-1962 Ruby red	1963 Cherry red	1964-1966 Black
Rear brake drum and hub	1938-1959 Amaranth red	1960-1962 Ruby red	1963 Cherry red	1964-1966 Black
Handlebars	1938-1951 Chrome	1952 Amaranth red	1953-1966 Chrome	
Voltage control unit	1938-1952 Black			
Rectifier	1952 Black	1953-1962 Light grey	1963-1966 self colour	
Electric horn	1938-1948 Black with chrome rim	1949-1961 Black	1962-1966 Silver cadmium plated	

AMAL CARBURETTOR SETTINGS

Year	Type	Bore (in)	Main Jet	Needle	Needle Jet	Position	Throttle Valve	Float Chamber	Pilot Jet
1938 to 1946	276 LH	15/16	140	6	.107	3	6/3	LH	–
1947 to 1948	276 RH BN/1AT	15/16	140	6	.107	3	6/3	RH	–
1949 to 1954	276 RH DK/1AT	15/16	140	6	.107	3	6/3^1/2	RH	–
1955 to 1958	376/25 Mono-bloc.	15/16	200	C	.1065	3	3^1/2	–	30
1959 to 1966	375/35 Mono-bloc.	7/8	160	B	.1065	3	3	–	25

OVERALL GEAR RATIOS
1938 to 1949 GEARBOX

Gears	Standard				Wide ratio				Close ratio			
	4th	3rd	2nd	1st	4th	3rd	2nd	1st	4th	3rd	2nd	1st
Engine Sprocket												
17	6.46	7.75	11.35	16.40	6.46	9.36	14.83	19.82	6.46	7.08	9.32	11.2
18	6.10	7.33	10.5	15.50	6.10	8.84	14.0	18.7	6.10	6.68	8.78	10.58
19	5.8	6.95	10.0	14.70	5.8	8.4	13.3	17.8	5.8	6.35	8.35	10.08
20	5.5	6.6	9.50	14.00	5.5	7.96	12.62	16.88	5.5	6.02	7.92	9.54
21	5.24	6.28	9.05	13.3	5.24	7.6	12.02	16.08	5.24	5.74	7.55	9.08
22	5.00	6.0	8.65	12.7	5.00	7.25	11.48	15.34	5.00	5.48	7.2	8.67
23	4.78	5.75	8.26	12.1	4.78	6.93	11.0	14.7	4.78	5.24	6.88	8.36
24	4.57	5.49	8.03	11.6	4.57	6.63	10.49	14.03	4.57	5.01	6.58	7.93
Gearbox Reduction	1.00	1.2	1.73	2.54	1.00	1.45	2.3	3.07	1.00	1.095	1.44	1.733

1950 to 1958 GEARBOX

Gears	Standard				Wide ratio				Close ratio			
	4th	3rd	2nd	1st	4th	3rd	2nd	1st	4th	3rd	2nd	1st
Engine Sprocket												
17	6.46	7.7	10.94	15.8	6.46	9.22	14.3	18.85	6.46	7.06	8.42	11.0
18	6.10	7.28	10.32	14.9	6.10	8.7	13.5	17.8	6.10	6.66	7.95	10.4
19	5.8	6.9	9.8	14.15	5.8	8.25	12.8	16.85	5.8	6.32	7.54	9.84
20	5.5	6.55	9.3	13.4	5.5	7.84	12.18	16.0	5.5	6.0	7.15	9.35
21	5.24	6.24	8.85	12.8	5.24	7.46	11.58	15.25	5.24	5.72	6.81	8.9
22	5.00	5.95	8.45	12.2	5.00	7.13	11.05	14.55	5.00	5.45	6.5	8.5
23	4.78	5.69	8.09	11.69	4.78	6.82	10.6	13.9	4.78	5.23	6.23	8.12
24	4.57	5.45	7.75	11.2	4.57	6.54	10.14	13.35	4.57	5.0	5.96	7.78
Gearbox Reduction	1.00	1.19	1.69	2.44	1.00	1.42	2.21	2.91	1.00	1.09	1.30	1.695

1959 to 1966 GEARBOX

Gears	Standard			
	4th	3rd	2nd	1st
Gearbox Sprocket				
18	5.31	6.3	9.32	13.00
19	5.05	6.0	8.9	12.3
20	4.8	5.62	8.35	11.56
Gearbox Reduction	1.00	1.17	1.74	2.41

CHAINS

Primary

Year	Size	Number of links	
		Solo	Sidecar
1938-1954	5/16" x 1/2"	78	77
1955-1958	5/16" x 1/2"	70	68
1959-1966	1/4" x 3/8" DUPLEX	78	—

Secondary

Year	Size	No. of links
1938-1954	3/8" x 5/8"	92
1955-1958	3/8" x 5/8"	100
1959-1964	3/8" x 5/8"	101
1964-1965	3/8" x 5/8"	104
1966	3/8" x 5/8"	103

SPEED TWIN

NOTABLE REGISTRATION NUMBERS

CKV 59 Factory registered *Motor Cycling* road test machine, October 1937
CVC 750 Factory registered *Motor Cycle* road test machine, October 1937
EDU 224 Maudes Trophy award machine, March 1939
EXR 3 Sir Malcolm Campbell's Speed Twin 1939
ERW 36 Factory registered *Motor Cycle* road test machine, November 1939
ENX 673 Factory registered *Motor Cycling* road test machine, January 1946
FUE 870 Factory registered *Motor Cycle* road test machine, August 1947
HHP 90 International Six Day Trial machine, September 1948 – rider A. Jefferies
HHP 91 International Six Day Trial machine, September 1948 – rider P. Alves
HHP 92 International Six Day Trial machine, September 1948 – rider B. Gaymer
HUE 552 Factory registered *Motor Cycling* road test machine, March 1949
KWD 457 Factory demonstrator/loan machine, 1949
LYV 222 Automobile Association combination, 1950
NAC 288 Factory registered *Motor Cycle* road test machine, March 1953
RNX 592 Factory registered *Motor Cycle* road test machine, May 1955
698 AAC Factory registered *Motor Cycle* road test machine, January 1959
239 BUE Factory registered Speed Twin, 1959

5T SHOW MODELS

Listed below are the engine/frame numbers of Speed Twin models built for various shows that the company supported throughout the years.

TF 15216/88793

Built 11.9.1947 for Paris Show as 1948 model fitted with a spring wheel.

TF 23951/101198

Built 16.9.1948 for Paris Show as 1949 fitted with a spring wheel.

TF 25372/101935
TF 25373/102460
TF 25374/102162
TF 25375/102163
TF 25376/102521
TF 25377/101933
TF 25378/102161
TF 25379/101220
TF 25380/101934

Built 12.11.1948 for Earls Court London Show as 1949 models. Only the first three were fitted with a spring wheel

TF 29510/102522

Built 13.4.1949 for works showroom, fitted with a spring wheel.

1009 N
1010 N
1011 N
1012 N
1013 N
1014 N
1015 N
1016 N

Built 8.10.1949 for Earls Court London Show as 1950 models. All fitted with a spring wheel.

1066 N

Built 10.10.1949 for Paris Show as a 1950 model. Fitted with a spring wheel.

13725 NA 13726 NA	Built 19.9.1951 for Frankfurt Show as a 1952 model. Fitted with a spring wheel.
14663 NA 14664 NA 14665 NA 14666 NA 14667 NA	Built 5.10.1951 for Earls Court London Show as a 1952 model. All fitted with a spring wheel.
15764 NA	Built 31.10.1951 for Earls Court London Show as a 1952 model. Fitted with a spring wheel.
29280 29292	Built 11.6.1952 for Canadian Show as a 1952 model. Fitted with a spring wheel.
33223 33224	Built 23.9.1952 for Paris Show as a 1953 model. Fitted with a spring wheel.
34059 34060 34061 34062 34063	Built 20.10.1952 for Earls Court London Show as 1953 models. Only the first two were fitted with a spring wheel.
34406 s/w 34407 s/w 34408 34410 34412 34413 34414 34416 s/w 34417 34418 34419 34420 34421	Built 5.11.1952 for Earls Court London Show as 1953 models. Only those indicated by s/w were fitted with a spring wheel.
34430 34447 34448 34451	Built 7.11.1952 for Earls Court London Show as 1953 models. All were fitted with a spring wheel.
35361 35362 35363	Built 8.12.1952 for Philippine Islands Show as 1953 models. Fitted with a spring wheel.
45578 45579	

45580 45581 45582 45583	Built 6.10.1953 for Earls Court London Show as 1954 models. Fitted with a spring wheel.
58990 58991 58992 58994	Built 6.11.1954 for Earls Court London Show as 1955 models
58993	Built 9.12.1954 for works showroom as a 1955 model.
60693 60694	Built 24.11.1954 for Brussels Show as 1955 models.
62089 62090	Built 5.1.1955 for Amsterdam Show as 1955 models.
71642 71643 71644 71645	Built 15.9.1955 for Earls Court London Show as 1956 models.
71827	Built 20.9.1955 for Paris Show as a 1956 model.
73883 73884	Built 10.11.1955 for Brussels Show as 1956 models.
02064 02065 02066	Built 25.9.1956 for Earls Court London Show as 1957 models.
02911 02912	Built 24.10.1956 for Milan Show as 1957 models.
011072 011073	Built 6.9.1957 for Paris Show with magneto and dynamo as police specification.
011858	Built 21.10.1957 for Milan Show as a 1958 model
011961	Built 24.10.1957 for Venezuela Show with magneto and dynamo as police specification.
013267	Built 9.12.1957 for works showroom as a 1958 model.

5TA SHOW MODELS

H5483 H5484	Built 17.9.1958 for Earls Court London Show as 1959 models.
H6187	Built 3.10.1958 for Earls Court London Show as a 1959 model.
H12614	Built 22.10.1959 for USA Show as a 1960 model.
H1811	Built 22.8.1960 for Paris Show as a 1961 model.
H18627 H18628	Built 1.9.1960 for Earls Court London Show as 1961 models.
H18638 H18639	Built 24.10.1960 for Earls Court London Show as 1961 models. These two were not built to show finish.
H30289	Built 1.11.1962 for Earls Court London Show as a 1963 model.
H35134 H35135	Built 11.5.1964 for Tel-Aviv Show as standard 1964 models.
H36072	Built 12.9.1964 for Earls Court London Show as 1965 model.
H36716	Built 28.10.1964 for Earls Court London Show as 1965 model.
H42227	Built 8.9.1965 for Earls Court London Show as 1966 model.

PARTS SERVICEABILITY

As a result of running a 1947 Speed Twin for 83,221 miles the Triumph Experimental
Department recorded the following failures:

Engine	Miles
Main bearing R.H.	36214, 48300
Main bearing L.H.	48236
Piston Rings	12032, 48300, 72000
Head Gasket	12032, 48300, 72000
Cylinder Head	72000 valve seats sunk
Valves	48300, 72000
Valve springs	12032, 48300, 72000
Valve guides	48300, 72000
Magneto	3630, 54420, 75260
Auto advance unit	47575 seized
Dynamo	52717, 64805, 75260
Gearbox	
High gear bush	53307
Layshaft 2nd gear	75043 broken tooth
Chains	
Primary	14138, 18472, 23357, 34996, 52599
Secondary	12832, 18472, 41894, 51552
Clutch	
Corked plates	11168, 26774
Wheels	
Bearings front	32907
Brake linings – front	48326, 67525
Brake linings – rear	58743
Tyre front	22839, 32906, 43720, 66400, 79646
Tyre rear	16112, 22840, 44485, 54597, 64790, 76570
Frame	
Rear	12353 saddle spring lug fractured
Petrol tank	42898 fractured
Clutch Cable	44185, 71306
Throttle Cable	21021, 43780

Electrical
    Ammeter   26326, 79246, 79400
    Battery   23636, 83321
Speedometer   11933, 12832, 14100, 49999, 50884, 52301,
                                   71921
    Speedometer Drive Gearbox   13875

From this summary it will be seen that some components, generally not of Triumph manufacture, have a higher incidence of failure and as this was a company mileage machine its useage would have been fairly hard. It is not suggested that a privately-owned Speed Twin would show the same regularity of failures but it still gives an indication of what long term ownership may represent.